FIELD & STREAM

RIFLE GUIDE

RIFLE SKILLS YOU NEED

DAVID E. PETZAL
AND THE EDITORS OF *FIELD & STREAM*

weldon**owen**

CONTENTS

01 FOLLOW THE BASIC SAFETY RULES

If you've been shooting for any time at all and had any kind of proper education (by which we mean anything from a firearms certification class to a big brother who slapped you upside the head for acting stupid), you should know these rules. We're reminding you here because it never hurts to be reminded, and because reading it together is a great starting point for a discussion about safety with a kid or any other new shooter.

ASSUME EVERY GUN IS LOADED Every time you see a gun, pick up a gun, or point a gun, always assume that it's loaded, and treat it accordingly.

CARRY SAFELY Make sure your safety is always on and that the barrel is pointing down when you are walking with or transporting your gun.

BE SURE OF YOUR TARGET Be absolutely sure that you are shooting at an animal and not a human, and that no people are anywhere near the animal you are shooting at. Never shoot at just a sound or movement.

DRESS RIGHT Wear at least the required amount of orange so that you don't become another hunter's target.

CONFIRM YOUR KILL Make sure all animals are dead before you put them in or strap them onto your vehicle.

BE KID SMART Do not bring small children hunting with you. Wait until your kids are old enough to understand and follow all of these rules before you take them out hunting.

CLIMB CAREFULLY Do not climb up or down a tree or over a fence or any other obstacle with a loaded gun.

KEEP YOUR FINGER CLEAR Make sure your finger stays off the trigger until you're ready to shoot.

SHOOT SOBER Alcohol and firearms don't mix; it's just plain common sense. Save those beers until the end of the day.

REMEMBER RANGE Look well beyond your target before you shoot. High-powered ammunition can travel up to three miles and still be deadly.

BUDDY UP Hunt with a buddy. If you can't, then at least make sure that someone knows where you will be and a time to expect you back.

STRAP IN If you're using a tree stand to hunt, don't forget to wear a safety belt. A lot of hunting injuries involve falling from a tree stand. You really don't want to have to tell the guys at work that's how you broke your arm.

CHECK IT OUT Before you begin the hunting season and before you use any new or borrowed equipment, make sure to go over everything and make sure that it is working properly. Make sure you know how everything operates before you attempt to use it while hunting.

STORE SAFE Store and transport ammunition separate from your guns. Keep everything secured under lock and key when it's not in use.

02 BUY YOUR KID A RIFLE

Watch a kid play a video game, and it's easy to tell why my recommendation for his first gun is a single-shot .22. The majority of these rifles will be bolt actions, and they'll serve you and your offspring well. Here are some thing to consider.

STAY STEADY A rifle needs to be a lot more than just a way to make mountains of shell casings. The single-shot forces him to load one round at a time, which encourages him to not waste that round when sending it downrange.

KNOW YOUR TARGET Show me a kid shooting a .22 with a larger-capacity magazine, and I'll show you a kid who'll use every one of those rounds to hit his target. There's no need to aim if he can just pour dozens of shots in the general vicinity. With a single-shot rifle, he'll consider every cartridge he uses.

SAVE YOUR MONEY A brick of .22 cartridges won't set you back terribly much. But the habits that kid forms with this first rifle will follow him the rest of his life. Teach him not to be wasteful now, and it'll save him in the long run.

RESPECT THE RIFLE It's not a toy, and it's your job to teach him that fact. There's no reset button on a rifle. A mistake here can kill someone.

DO DOUBLE DUTY The single-shot .22 will be great for learning range basics and plinking. And since most youngsters start off in the field hunting small game, the .22 is an obvious first choice to develop their skills and learn good habits in hunting.

Rifles are exceedingly simple machines with very few moving parts. However, just like computers or automobiles, they have their own jargon, which you must master if you are to learn about them. This is the basic nomenclature. Learn it, and the next time someone uses the phrase "lock, stock, and barrel," you can explain its derivation. Isn't that worth the effort?

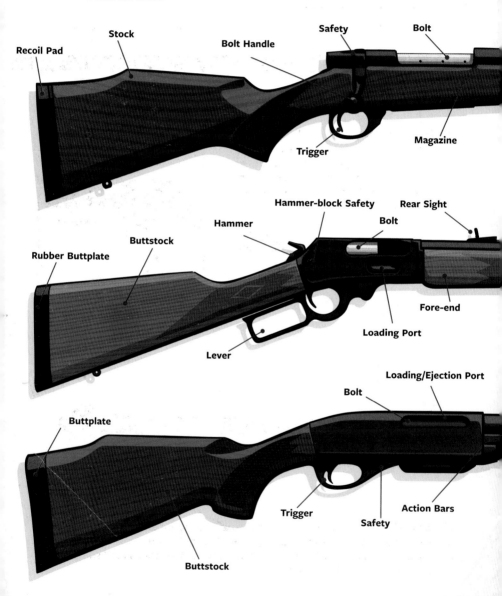

Stock
Recoil Pad
Bolt Handle
Safety
Bolt
Trigger
Magazine

Hammer-block Safety
Rear Sight
Hammer
Bolt
Buttstock
Rubber Buttplate
Fore-end
Loading Port
Lever

Loading/Ejection Port
Bolt
Buttplate
Action Bars
Trigger
Safety
Buttstock

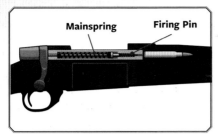

Mainspring **Firing Pin**

BOLT ACTION The bolt action remains the strongest and most versatile of all rifle actions, and is the foundation for our most accurate rifles. The bolt cycles with four movements: up, back, forward, and down.

Barrel **Muzzle**

LEVER ACTION Highly reliable, this design requires only a quick down/up pull on the lever to shuck out an empty cartridge, feed in a new one, and cock the hammer. Levers are not as strong as bolts, and the top-ejecting versions are not compatible with scopes.

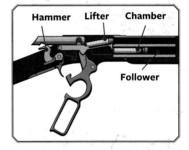

Hammer **Lifter** **Chamber**

Follower

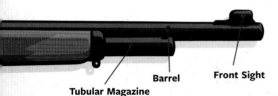

Barrel **Front Sight**

Tubular Magazine

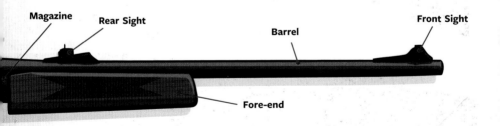

Magazine **Rear Sight**

Barrel

Front Sight

Fore-end

PUMP ACTION The pump, or slide, action shares the speed and simplicity of the lever action but is considerably stronger. In addition, it works well with modern cartridges and scope sights. To use, you just pull back on the fore-end and slam it forward, and you're ready to shoot again.

04 BUILD YOUR HOME GUN BENCH

While I leave major jobs to a gunsmith, I like to be able to take guns apart and put them back together, mount scopes, switch stock shims, and so on myself. My gun bench contains the following:

THE BASICS

- A gun cradle to hold guns so I can work on them with both hands

- A Phillips-head screwdriver for removing recoil pads

- A large flat-head screwdriver for removing stock bolts

- Mini versions of both flat- and Phillips-head screwdrivers

- A socket wrench with extension for removing stock bolts that don't have slotted heads

- A spanner made for removing pump-action forearms

- A set of roll pin punches

- A set of gunsmithing screwdrivers with interchangeable heads so I don't mar any screws

- Loctite (blue) for scope mounting

- Scope levels

- Allen and Torx wrenches for scope mounting

- Brass/nylon hammer for tapping without denting

- Vise-grip pliers for grabbing things that are really stuck or for holding small parts while I butcher them

- A set of jeweler's screwdrivers for very small screws

- A Leatherman Wave multi-tool, mostly for its needle-nose pliers

- A complete set of hex wrenches

- A trigger-pull scale

ON MY WISH LIST:

- Brownell's padded magazine cap pliers

- A Hawkeye Bore Scope that connects with a TV screen so I can really get a good look inside a barrel

I AM ALWAYS OUT OF:

- Spray cans of compressed air

- Birchwood Casey Gun Scrubber

CLEANING AND LUBRICATING SUPPLIES

- Cleaning rods with phosphor-bronze brushes and wool mops in all gauges (10-gauge brushes make good 12-gauge chamber brushes)

- Old toothbrush

- Round brushes

- Plastic pick (looks like a dental tool)

- Cotton patches

- Rags

- #0000 grade steel wool

- Shooter's Choice Grease for hinge pins and magazine cap threads

- Birchwood Casey Choke Tube grease

- Gun oil in spray cans and bottles (not WD-40)

- Birchwood Casey Gun Scrubber or Liquid Wrench for thorough action cleanings

- Spray can of powder solvent for bore cleaning

- A box of Q-tips

- A can of lighter fluid for small degreasing jobs

- Lens tissues and a bottle of lens cleaner for cleaning scope lenses

- A jar of Brownell's Action Lube (pretty much the same stuff as choke-tube grease)

- A bottle of clear nail polish for freezing trigger screws in place

- Many jars of J-B Non-Embedding Bore Cleaning Compound

- Shooter's Choice Powder Solvent

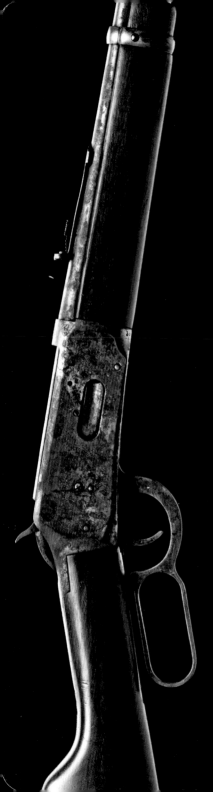

COMBAT RUST

Bluing, by itself, is not protection. Bluing is created by controlled rusting, and its only contribution in the fight against corrosion is its ability to retain oil.

Oil prevents rust, but not for long. If you're interested in serious protection for your firearm, a very thin coat of floor wax works better than oil, particularly on the bottom of the barrel and receiver where they are in contact with the stock.

Body chemistry also causes guns to rust. This occurs via fingerprints; it's why you see arms-collection curators handling their treasures with white gloves. Some people's fingerprints are positively poisonous; other folks can grope guns forever without leaving a speck of the red stuff.

Stainless steel is not immune to rust. That's because the "stainless" steel used in firearms is not truly stainless. It will rust the same as chrome-moly; it just takes a little bit longer.

Dirty guns will rust faster, and rust worse, than clean guns. This is because dirt attracts and holds on to moisture.

Light surface rust can sometimes be removed by rubbing gently with 0000 steel wool and Shooter's Choice Powder Solvent. If actual pits have formed, a gunsmith will have to polish them out and reblue the afflicted part. And if the pits are deep enough, too bad; you're just gonna have to live with them.

Storing guns where air cannot circulate is like setting out a big WELCOME mat for rust. Some prime examples are storing guns in a vinyl case that can't breathe, or plugging the barrel with grease at one or both ends. The new "freeze-dry" storage cases, from which you pump out all the air, are the exception to this rule.

If you're hunting in a heavy rain and decide to put off wiping down your rifle at the end of the day until you've had a cup of warm milk or two, you may find yourself with a hell of a case of rust. Your rifle comes first, always.

06 KEEP IT CLEAN

Some time ago, I was asked how to clean a rifle. There are as many different ways to do this as there are to summon Beelzebub, and there is no single "correct" method. Whatever works, works. Think of the cleaning as a two-stage process. First you get out the powder fouling and then you get out the copper.

For powder fouling, I use Shooter's Choice solvent and phosphor-bronze brushes. When you're finished with a brush, give it a good shot with a can of Birchwood Casey Gun Scrubber; this will get the dirt off the brush and will keep the Shooter's Choice from eating away at the bronze bristles.

07 DEAL WITH POWDER FOULING

CLEAN YOUR BORE For copper fouling, I use J-B Non-Embedding Bore Cleaning Compound. Other copper-killers will not work on some barrels, or take forever, or will pit your bore if you leave them in too long. This stuff works fast and will get all the copper out for sure.

KEEP YOUR RODS CLEAN This is why God gave us paper towels. A dirty rod is an instrument of destruction.

SKIP SLOT-TYPE PATCH HOLDERS You do not want to drag dirty patches back and forth through the bore. Each patch gets one trip only.

BE SURE When you think you're done, leave the bore wet with Shooter's Choice for a couple of hours and then run a dry patch through. If it comes out with no green on it, you're done. Then run a Rem-Oil patch through the bore and a dry one after it to finish the job.

CLEAN THE CHAMBER Use a dry patch to swab it out. You don't want anything left in there when you're done.

08 SPEND SMART

Extensive work on firearms, older ones in particular, should be thought out very carefully. If you have an innacurate rifle, working on it may not make it a shooter. With so many incredibly accurate guns available right out of the box, my attitude these days is that if it doesn't shoot, sell it. Most old guns are not worth redoing. Leave them alone and accept their scars and dings as badges of honor. That said, you may possess guns that have a sentimental value and wish to improve their appearance. Such work does not increase the gun's worth to a collector but nonetheless enhances the owning experience to you. If that's the case, go right ahead.

09 CURE A SICK TRIGGER

From the 1980s until about 2000, rifle makers routinely put out guns that were excellent—except for the trigger. Today's triggers are infinitely better, but there are still plenty of dogs out there. If you shoot less than a box of ammo a year and take your rifle out of the case only during deer season, don't worry about your trigger—you're not a serious shooter. But if you don't shoot well, want to improve, and your trigger is part of the problem, you can adjust or replace it. A gunsmith will take it completely apart, polish the engaging surfaces, and/ or replace the spring that controls the pull weight. He or she may also tell you that nothing can be done with your trigger, and that might be true. You can replace it with a much better model for a good price. If you are a serious shooter and/or have a fine rifle that you would like to turn into a supergun, you will not begrudge a penny that you spend.

10 KEEP YOUR GUN HAPPY

The tragedy of rifle neglect (like dandruff or flatulence) occurs in even the finest people. But that doesn't make it right. Your rifle wants to be your friend and will perform faithfully for you. All it needs to succeed at this is some careful but cheap attention, outlined in these 10 steps.

SCRUB THE BARREL Scrub away with powder solvent, patches, and a phosphor-bronze brush, and then polish all of the little grooves and lands with J-B Non-Embedding Bore Cleaning Compound. When you can no longer see copper streaks from the muzzle end, you're done.

FIX THE DINGS Major dents in a wood-stocked rifle can often be raised by laying a damp cleaning patch over the depression and heating the cloth with the tip of a hot iron. The steam will work its way into the wood fibers, causing them to swell, and the dent will either diminish or vanish.

HOSE DOWN THE ACTION Get a can of Birchwood Casey Gun Scrubber. Next, take your barreled action out of its stock and remove the scope. (If you have a lever or pump or auto, remove the buttstock.) Now, spray down the action, and in the case of a bolt gun, the trigger as well. The most amazing stuff will come out. Do not re-oil. I will say that again: Do not re-oil.

REMOVE THE GOO While the barreled action is out of the stock, wipe off all the accumulated goo that's on the underside of the barrel and the receiver. Do this to the corresponding surfaces in the stock as well. Re-oil the metal surfaces you've just cleaned. Lightly.

INSPECT THE BASE While the scope is off the rifle, make sure the base screws are tight. If you're really conscientious, remove the bases and check for oil that's seeped underneath. Wipe it off. Degrease all surfaces, including the base screws and screw holes, and replace the bases. Be sure the screws are as tight as they were before.

CLEAN YOUR SCOPE LENSES Treat your delicate optics kindly; use camera lens cleaning solution and lens tissue. You can find them at any photo-supply store.

REMOVE RUST Light rust can be removed by scrubbing with 0000 steel wool and a little oil. A rusted trigger is a more serious problem; a gunsmith will have to take it apart and clean it or replace it.

REBLUE WORN AREAS Some shooters consider bright spots to be the equivalent of campaign ribbons. I do, to an extent. But they are more likely to rust than blued surfaces, so you may want to get rid of them with a bottle of gun blue.

REPLACE BURRED SCREWS The best way to get new ones is from a gunsmith. They can sell you the exact number and size you need. This includes not only ring and base screws but also bedding screws.

UPGRADE TO TORX Even if your slot- or hex-head base and ring screws are not damaged, consider replacing them with Torx screws. You can drive the suckers in tight and they are almost impossible to bugger up, even by the most ham-handed people. Base screws should be tightened until blood starts seeping from under your fingernails. The ring screws should be tightened firmly, not obsessively, because you may have to take your scope off in the field, where a screw that won't budge is the last thing you need.

11 DON'T BE THAT GUY

You're ready to go, with the latest and greatest gear, you're carrying the latest and greatest rifle or shotgun, and you're off to hit the woods to give the game what for. Before you take one step onto the hunt, however, stop and make sure you aren't making a fool of yourself.

CHOOSE THE RIGHT CAMO We have camo up the kazoo, but it's all Southern—southern swamps, southern oaks, southern kudzu, and southern highway litter. You won't find Dismal Swamp in Wyoming.

KNOCK OFF THE SHINE When the whole world is brainwashed by camo, why do shiny rifles still sell? You might like shiny, but animals will see it and think, "Why die when I can run?"

FORGET "BREATHABLE" Those cool clothes are fine until you start to hustle. Then you'll be roasted in your own juices. Down, synthetic insulation, and oiled cotton will feel like a Dutch oven.

GET A WHIFF There are tons of ads for poly underwear "treated to resist odor-causing bacteria." Don't believe a word of it. And don't waste your money.

GET ANOTHER WHIFF Deer scents may be the cat's meow for bowhunters who have to work up close and personal, but they're just silly for the rest of us.

TRUMP TECHNOLOGY WITH SKILL A hunter used to be a person who acquired a broad variety of skills by spending tons of time in the woods and working very hard at his craft. Now, the assumption is that you can bypass much of the process if you spend enough money. There's no substitute for know-how, so get out there and learn.

RESPECT THE GAME Killing is a part of hunting, but hunting is not simply killing. There is only one way to look at an animal you have just killed, and that is in sorrow. People who hate hunting will never believe or understand that, but who cares?

12 ACCESS YOUR LIZARD BRAIN

Rifle shooting is a great many different things, ranging from slow, calculated precision work at long range to fast shooting at point-blank range. To excel at one (or both), you need a reptilian nervous system. It is to all other factors as three is to one.

If you can't stomp on your nerves, you will never be able to shoot a rifle well. I've known two men who could not shoot and could not be taught to shoot. The problem with both was not their eyes or their hands or their shoulders; it was their psyches.

Gifted shooters, on the other hand, are able to tap into their lizard brains, which make them immune to whatever devils beset the rest of us. They can shoot under intense pressure. This can mean anything from an African professional hunter sticking a bullet in a buffalo's eye just as old nyati is about to get a horn into him to an Olympic shooter not blowing it when she needs one more squeeze of the trigger to secure the gold medal. Whatever the situation, they know that when they pick up a rifle they are going to hit whatever they aim at, period.

13 DON'T BE STUPID

In almost every situation, some basic rules apply. If you're going for the larger, more dangerous prey, all the more reason to review your fundamentals. Get to the range and burn some ammo. Doing so will at least keep you from making the following four mistakes:

MISTAKE ONE Finding out the hard way that you can't shoulder your rifle because what you are wearing out there in cold moose country is so thick that you can't get the scope close enough to get a proper sight picture.

MISTAKE TWO Sighting in your rifle with the scope on 10X and leaving it there instead of returning to 4X.

MISTAKE THREE Forgetting where your safety is, or how the thing works, or that you even have a safety.

MISTAKE FOUR Keeping the rifle slung over your shoulder, or worse, across your back as you hike across the tundra in search of moose.

14 SPEND YOUR MONEY WISELY

There are only three rational courses to pursue when buying a rifle:

ONE If all you can afford is a cheap gun, get a good cheap gun, get it a trigger job if it needs one, and let it alone.

TWO If you want something classy but don't have thousands of dollars to buy a true custom working rifle, save up your pennies until you have about half that amount and get a Kimber Model 84, or a Weatherby Mark V, or a Nosler Model 48 Trophy Grade, or a Sako Model 85, or three or four others that I can't call to mind right now. Are these rifles really worth twice as much as guns that cost, say, $800? Yes. Will you be tempted to "improve" them? Only if you've got serious brain damage.

THREE If you want to go whole hog and get a rifle from D'Arcy Achols, or New Ultra Light Arms, or the Remington Custom Shop, or Montana Rifles, or anyone in that exalted company, then you will want to think very long and hard before you even start saving. Much of what you are buying is intangible, and we will get into those details in another entry later on in this book.

15 TRY THE TRIGGER

Figuring out if you have a good trigger or a bad one is not rocket science. There are three important components to any trigger pull:

CREEP describes the movement of the trigger before it breaks and releases the sear, which releases the firing pin. Your trigger should have no creep at all: You pull and it should just go off.

WEIGHT OF PULL is the pounds and ounces of pressure it takes to make the trigger break.

OVERTRAVEL is the distance the trigger moves after it breaks. If there is excess overtravel, it will disturb your follow-through after you shoot.

16 KNOW WHY SHORTER IS BETTER

For a big-game rifle barrel, I think the most practical length is 22 inches. If you have a magnum, 24 is the most you want, and you can get away with 23 inches unless you're shooting something like a 7mm Shooting Times Westerner.

I've found that whatever small ballistic advantage you gain with a barrel over 24 inches is more than offset by the added weight and length. About a year ago, I grew fed up with the 26-inch barrel on a .338 Remington Ultra Magnum Model 700 and had it cut back to 23½ inches.

Despite the huge charge of slow powder in this cartridge, I lost only 38 fps, and accuracy improved dramatically (which often happens, but not always, when you cut down a barrel).

I have only two rifles with 26-inch barrels. One is a .220 Swift, from which I want all the velocity I can get and other considerations come second. The other is a .300 Weatherby, which I reserve for situations when I know I'm going to take long shots or none at all, and I won't have to carry the thing around very much.

17 TAKE STOCK

When it comes to picking out a stock, you have three basic categories to choose from:

COMPOSITE Most composite stocks are made of fiberglass reinforced with other materials such as graphite and/or Kevlar. They tend to be expensive because they are built one at a time, by hand. But they are terrific stocks. A few composites are made of Kevlar and graphite; they are the lightest and strongest of all, but they are definitely going to be quite expensive.

FIBERGLASS Outmoded for fly rods but makes a terrific stock. Very strong, light, dead stable, and not as expensive as some other stock types. You can even get the paint "integral" with the fiberglass, which means you can polish out scratches with fine steel wool. Army and marine sniper rifles employ fiberglass stocks.

LAMINATED WOOD Very strong and, if properly sealed, very stable as well. Laminated stocks can be made of one type of wood or of several types and left natural colored or stained. Some are quite good looking. This type of stock is often preferred by shooters who are looking for strength and stability but regard a "plastic" stock as they would a venomous reptile.

18 WEIGH YOUR OPTIONS

In rifle design, everything is a trade-off. When you remove weight, you make a rifle easier to carry, but you also make it harder to hold steady, and sometimes you need steady very badly. Years ago in Colorado, I was hunting elk at 8,000 feet and spotted a 5x5 bull uphill from me. The only way I could get a shot at the unfortunate ungulate was to sprint 40 yards nearly straight up to a little plateau.

Since sprinting 4 yards on the flat at sea level is an effort for me, I was on the verge of having a coronary by the time I got into shooting position, but I was nonetheless able to aim, courtesy of the 9¼-pound .338 I was carrying. It was no fun to lug around, but it remained steady even when my chest was heaving like a bellows.

Recoil is also affected. A light rifle, chambered for a hard-kicking cartridge, will pummel you. The only way to avoid this is to use a muzzle brake, which creates problems of its own, including added length and weight and an inhuman ear-shattering muzzle blast.

Based on my own experience, here's a rough guide to what big-game rifles should weigh with scope aboard:

.243 up through .270: 6½ to 7 pounds

.30/06 through the .30 magnums: 7½ to 9 pounds

.338 Winchester, .338 Remington Ultra Magnum, .340 Weatherby, .375 Holland & Holland: 9 to 10 pounds

.416 Remington or larger: 9½ to 12 pounds

19 CHECK THE BASICS

Congratulations on your new rifle, and I wish you much joy in your relationship. I trust that you haven't bought anything that is shiny, or too heavy, or too light, or that kicks more than you can handle. If all that is in good order, then your next step is to find out how well the thing actually shoots—or doesn't.

First, you want to weigh the trigger with a spring gauge, or ask your gunsmith to do it. It should break at not less than 3 pounds and no more than 4. Some very good modern factory triggers require no work at all, but there are also a lot of dogs. If yours barks, it's time to go to the gunsmith. There's no getting around this. A bad trigger on a rifle is a lot like bad steering in a car.

At the range, load the magazine and ensure that the rifle feeds reliably. A surprising number don't, particularly those chambered for short, fat cartridges. If your gun is a bolt action, don't work the bolt timidly; slam it back and forth. That's the way they're designed to be used. It should go through chambering, firing, extracting, and ejecting without a hitch. If it doesn't, send it back to the factory or take it to a gunsmith. Or you can take it out hunting and hope that it will work.

Next, you're going to want to check for accuracy. Make sure that the scope-base and bedding screws are properly tightened. These are often installed by uncaring hourly-wage workers, and you can save yourself lots of grief with just a few turns of your screwdriver.

Speaking of pain and woe, don't mount your scope unless you know how to do it correctly. This is such a problem that two gunmakers I know refuse to sell their rifles unless they perform this job. Have your gunsmith do it instead.

The more precisely you can aim, the more accurately you'll shoot. Generally, you want to have at least 8X available, but personally, I like 9X or 10X a lot better, and on varmint rifles I consider 20X the minimum. Make sure your scope actually works while you're at it.

More than once I've seen cases in which a gun seemed to just go haywire, but it was actually the scope's fault. It's easy to spot one with loose adjustments or a busted reticle: The point of impact won't move up or down or right or left with any consistency, and the rifle it's mounted on won't group at all. Few guns, no matter how accuracy-impaired, won't give you some kind of group if the scope works.

BOLT ACTION By far the most popular action among hunters, the bolt-action rifle is opened and closed manually by lifting and pulling a protruding handle that looks similar to a door bolt. Closing the bolt chambers a fresh round, which is lifted from a magazine located underneath the action. Strong and dependable, the bolt action is very accurate.

LEVER ACTION The familiar cowboy gun of the American West, the lever action is worked by pulling down on a lever located at the trigger and then returning it to a locked position. These guns are surging in popularity due to new cartridge designs that allow for aerodynamic polycarbonate-tip bullets to be used in the tubular magazines.

PUMP A pump rifles is operated by sliding the fore-end to the rear, which ejects the fired cartridge, and then sliding it forward, which chambers a new round. While pump rifles are not as popular as autoloading models, they do have a strong following in some regions, particularly in Pennsylvania, where hunting with an autoloading rifle is illegal.

SINGLE SHOT Single-shot rifles must be reloaded after every shot. Break-action single-shot rifles are opened at the breech for reloading. Other examples include the "falling block" single-shot action, in which the breech is opened by moving a lever on the underside of the gun. Single-shot rifles are very safe to operate, very accurate, and very strong.

MODERN SPORTING RIFLE
Built in the style of the original
M-16 military rifle, the modern
sporting rifle is essentially a
semiautomatic firearm with
an ergonomic stock and the
easily recognizable protruding
magazine that has long defined
military arms. Also called ARs
(Armalite made the first models
in the 1960s), these firearms are
actually not fully automatic.

SEMIAUTOMATIC Using a
small part of the gas created by
the combustion of a cartridge's
powder, semiautomatic rifles
automatically eject and chamber
cartridges with each pull of the
trigger. Also called "autoloaders,"
they offer quick follow-up shots
that don't require the shooter to
manipulate a bolt or lever.

21 TAKE IT FOR A TEST DRIVE

Once you know your rifle is basically sound, you'll want to pick your ammo. Let's say your new rifle is a .270. Choose from among 130-, 140-, or 150-grain bullets. What matters most is the type: Do you want tough, premium slugs for tough animals or the squishy, standard variety for squishy animals? When you decide, buy a box of each weight in the appropriate type and see which gives you the best groups.

You should do your shooting as early or as late in the day as possible. The more sun there is, the more mirage there is. Avoid wind. At 100 yards, anything short of a gale has little effect on big-game bullets, but strong air currents are fatal to rimfire accuracy and no help if you're trying for very small groups with a varmint rifle.

If you're shooting at a public range, pick a bench where you are not next to some dunce who thinks he is Rambo and is blasting away with a semiauto that spits empties at you. If this happens to me, I pin a tag that reads "leprosy patient" on my shirt. People tend to clear out of the area pretty quickly.

Don't let your barrel get so hot that you can't hold on to it. If an electrical outlet is handy, bring a fan along and stand the rifle in front of it for a few minutes. Or find some shade and stand it butt down, barrel up. It'll cool faster. Clean the barrel every 20 rounds.

YOUR GOALS:
- Get at least three (or if you're of a suspicious nature, go for five) consecutive three-shot groups of 1½ inches or less for a big-game rifle, and five-shot groups of ½ inch or less for a varmint gun or a .22. Shoot at 100 yards, except for rimfires, which should be shot at 25 yards. Really good big-game rifles should print groups of under an inch and varminters close to ¼ inch.
- There should be no fliers, which are errant shots that are not caused by pure shooter error.
- All the groups should be printing in the same place on the target.

That's it. If you want to sum up all of this advice in a single sentence, "Make sure the damn thing works" would do nicely. It's amazing how many people never take the trouble.

22 KNOW THE 10 BEST RIFLES EVER

1. Winchester Model 70 (pre-1964)
Created in 1936, Winchester advertised this gun as "the rifleman's rifle," and its features made for a powerful, efficient big-game hunting rifle that still lives up to the slogan.

2. Mauser Model 98
Made in military and sporting versions, the 98's action was the basis for nearly every bolt action since. A successful, sturdy weapon, the Mauser operates in even the harshest conditions.

3. Winchester Model 94
This rifle is light, fast, and reliable. Despite its relatively short range, it has little kick and carries easily. Favored in .30/30 caliber, this weapon is synonymous with the term "deer rifle."

4. Remington Model 700
First available in 1962, the 700 was based on the post-WWII model 721. This rifle is a great combination of simple design, excellent trigger, and incredible accuracy.

5. Ruger 10/22
Since 1964, this rimfire rifle has been one of the most popular and most customized designs ever. Various modifications allow the 10/22 to range from simple tin-can shooter to high-end target rifle.

6. Springfield Model 1903
Issued to soldiers in WWI, the '03 was graceful and accurate. Originally a military rifle, the very first sporting variant was made especially for President Theodore Roosevelt in 1909.

7. Remington Nylon 66
First offered in 1959, this rifle had a stock that was made with a brand-new synthetic called Zytel. Light and accurate, the 66 paved the way for future synthetic stocks.

8. New Ultra Light Arms Model 20
With its 1-pound Kevlar stock, this .308 caliber rifle weighs a mere $5\frac{1}{2}$ pounds with scope mounted and is just as accurate as much heavier guns.

9. Savage Model 110
Produced from 1958 onward, the first model 110s were unlovely, but they were inexpensive and accurate and are today offered in all manner of configurations.

10. Marlin Model 336
First sold in 1948, this is another great deer rifle like the Winchester 94—short, light, fast, reliable, and its side-ejection allows for a scope to be mounted as well.

23 CHOOSE YOUR METAL

Both stainless steel and chrome-moly make fine barrels. Chrome-moly can be blued, but stainless cannot. Stainless is somewhat more expensive but will last longer because it's more resistant to erosion from powder gas. No matter what it's made of, make sure you keep your barrel clean. You can have dirty thoughts, but your barrel should be spotless.

24 BUY IT FOR THE BARREL

A little while back I was talking with Chad Dixon, the gunsmith who builds Scimitar tactical rifles for Dakota Arms. Scimitars have to shoot five consecutive 10-shot groups that measure ½ inch or less before they leave the shop, so you could assume that Chad knows something about accuracy, and he said the following: "If someone wanted me to build him an accurate rifle, I would ask how much he had to spend, and then put 80 percent of that into the barrel. The rest I could improvise one way or another. Spend your money on the barrel."

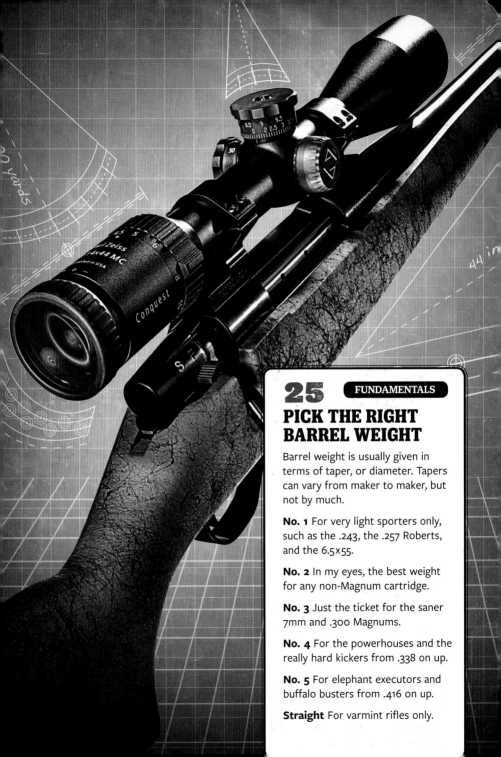

25   FUNDAMENTALS

PICK THE RIGHT BARREL WEIGHT

Barrel weight is usually given in terms of taper, or diameter. Tapers can vary from maker to maker, but not by much.

No. 1 For very light sporters only, such as the .243, the .257 Roberts, and the 6.5x55.

No. 2 In my eyes, the best weight for any non-Magnum cartridge.

No. 3 Just the ticket for the saner 7mm and .300 Magnums.

No. 4 For the powerhouses and the really hard kickers from .338 on up.

No. 5 For elephant executors and buffalo busters from .416 on up.

Straight For varmint rifles only.

26 KNOW WHY SHORTER IS BETTER, PART TWO

Back when men carried Kentucky rifles, long barrels were just the ticket—44 inches was about standard. They reduced aiming error and all the weight in front made offhand shooting much easier. Later, the shorter Hawken rifle evolved (26 to 38 inches), because its users had found that a long rifle was a damned unhandy thing to hunt with while on horseback. The most practical length for a big-game barrel is 22 inches. For a magnum, 24 is the most you want. You can get away with 23 unless you're shooting something like a 7mm STW. Twenty-six is okay with varmint guns, and 20 is fine on a rifle chambered for small rounds, like the .257 Roberts, .260, .308, or 7mm/08.

27 ROLL OUT THE BARREL

Most custom barrels are produced by a process called button rifling, which was developed in the 1950s and is reasonably fast, but not nearly as fast as hammering. In button rifling, a tungsten-carbide button with a reverse imprint of the rifling grooves is pulled through a blank by a hydraulic press. If done slowly and with care, this will produce a truly superior barrel.

Some custom barrel makers, including Douglas, Shaw, and McGowen, make highly affordable barrels that are better than what the factories put out. I've shot a whole bunch of these. The worst of them was good, and the best would suck the breath out of your lungs—they were that accurate. This class of barrel is the best choice for a hunting rifle because any gain in accuracy you'd obtain from a more expensive barrel would go unrealized in the field. The cost, including chambering, threading, polishing, and bluing (which are performed by your gunsmith), will probably be a few hundred bucks.

28 KNOW WHY IT WORKS

LOCK TIME is the interval between when the sear releases the firing pin and the primer ignites. Long lock times invite aiming errors, because you can flinch in those fractions of a second. Most modern bolt-action guns have fast lock times.

TRIGGERS If you have to haul on something that does not want to give, you are not going to shoot well.

THE BARREL must be straight, and its rifling grooves and lands must be of the same depth for the whole length of the bore. A maker of first-rate barrels is obliged to let the depths of his grooves vary no more than .0005 of an inch.

BEDDING Back in the good old days (up until the late 1950s), most rifle barrels were full-length bedded with a bit of upward pressure on the barrel to damp its vibrations. With a good, stable piece of wood and a stockmaker who knew what he was doing, it was a satisfactory system. If, however, the wood shrank or swelled, or the inletting was poorly done, the result was quite wretched.

The modern solution is to free-float the barrel—to bed it solidly to the end of the chamber and let the rest of it wave in the air. The theory is that since there's nothing to interfere with the tube, it will vibrate the same for every shot. For the most part, this theory works very well, especially with heavy barrels. But there is one drawback. The gap between the barrel and the barrel channel, if there's a lot of it, is ugly. I've seen free-floated barrels with enough room under them to start a small nutria ranch.

Some gunmakers believe in full fore-end contact. Melvin Forbes, who builds New Ultra Light Arms rifles, glass-beds his barrels to have complete contact (but no pressure) from action to fore-end. Since his stocks are made of Kevlar and graphite, and therefore don't shift, he doesn't have to worry about any warping, shrinking, or swelling.

STOCKS In the late 1970s, the first practical synthetic stocks made their appearance. Disdained by traditionalists, they were pretty crude looking, but they were stronger, lighter, stiffer, and unaffected by changes in humidity. For the first time, they gave rifle builders a truly stable platform to build on. Along with synthetic stocks came pillar bedding. In its simplest form, it consists of two thick aluminum tubes that are epoxied into the stock. The front and rear bedding screws pass through them, and the action tang and the front of the receiver rest on them, giving you complete metal-to-metal contact. You can't compress them no matter how hard you turn the screws.

29 JUSTIFY YOUR PURCHASE

There is no logical reason to buy a custom rifle. I love the things and use them almost exclusively, but there is nothing they can do that I couldn't get done by using a good factory rifle. So why bother? What are you actually buying?

EXPERTISE When you pay all that money, what you are really buying is the ideas and skills of the man who made the rifle. If you get one of Melvin Forbes' Ultra Lights, you purchase the 20 years he spent as a country gunsmith fixing other peoples' mistakes, along with the two years he spent supporting himself as a shop teacher while designing a rifle that weighed 5-and-change pounds with scope.

PERFECTION When custom rifles leave the shop, they are supposed to work perfectly. Not well, not good enough, perfectly. If they do not perform just right, they will be made to.

EXCLUSIVITY Not every honyak in camp will be carrying a rifle made by Mark Bansner, or Nosler, or Kenny Jarrett. This is important to more people than you would think.

PERFORMANCE You're buying the cutting edge—the last 1 percent that money can purchase. No factory trigger will pull as well as a Jewell. No factory barrel will quite equal a Lilja, a Schneider, or a Pac-Nor, to name three. No factory stock has the uncanny light weight and strength of a High Tech Specialties stock.

If some or all of these factors are important to you, start saving your money.

30 KNOW YOUR GUNSMITH

Some gun builders will smile, take your money, and turn out exactly what you ordered, whether it's a crackpot gun or not. Others will tell you that you don't know what you're talking about. You want the latter. Any gunmaker with an ounce of pride does not want some screwball firearm out there with his name on it.

When you're shopping around for the right gunsmith, ask for the names of half a dozen of his customers and then find out if they like their guns. You will have to listen carefully. Some people are chronic malcontents; others have unrealistic expectations. A guy who couldn't hit water if he fell out of a boat is not a good reference for a gunmaker who guarantees

half-minute groups. The fact is that all top makers shoot their rifles before they go down the road, and they know they are accurate, and they are likely to be short with the customer who calls to complain that his gun won't deliver.

Once you choose your gunmaker, be sure to tell him how you're going to use the rifle. I recently had a 6.5x55 Swede built but neglected to tell the builder that I wanted to use long, heavy bullets. He assumed I'd follow the current trend for light, fast bullets and gave me a barrel with a 1-in-10½-inch twist—fine for light slugs but all wrong for heavy ones. I had to return the gun and get a new barrel. The whole thing was my fault.

31 ASSUME NOTHING

Just when you think you know everything, you get a lesson in humility. I have a very, very accurate .22 with a Lilja barrel that was installed by gunsmith John Blauvelt. After a while, the rifle wouldn't extract the fired brass. So I went whining to John and asked him to see what was wrong with the extractors. It turned out there was nothing wrong with them. Instead, when he put the bore scope up its bore, lo and behold there

was a disgusting ring of lead and burned powder near the front of the chamber. It had not been removed even by regular cleaning with a bronze-bristle .22 brush. It turns out that tight-chambered .22s often suffer from this type of loathsome deposit, and the way to get it out is to take a 6mm phospor-bronze brush and scrub the hell out of it. A .22 brush won't do because it doesn't fit tightly enough.

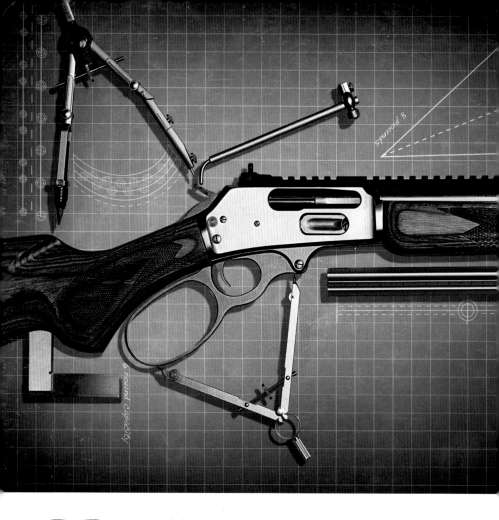

32 RESPECT YOUR TRIGGER

A trigger is to a rifle as steering is to a car. Steering that is too heavy or sloppy or gives you no feel of the road will have your car weaving all over the blacktop. Let me quote from *U.S. Army Field Manual 23-10, Sniper Training*: "Trigger control is the most important of the marksmanship fundamentals. It is defined as causing the rifle to fire when the sight picture is at its best *without causing the rifle to move* [italics mine]." If you have to wrestle your trigger, you're sunk, because your rifle will move.

If your trigger is a disgrace, you have two options: Have a gunsmith modify it or have him install a replacement. Usually, on a trigger that's not hopeless, an adjustment will cost you about $50.

It is, in fact, the case that some triggers are made so that they cannot be tampered with in any way. If this is your situation, you will need to get a replacement trigger, and there are several very good ones on the market these days, such as those from Timney, Jewell, and Rifle Basix.

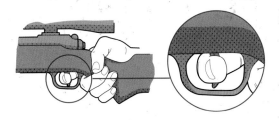

33
PULL IT
LIKE A PRO

FINGER TECHNIQUE Triggers are best pulled with the first joint of the index finger, not the soft tip of the finger. The "give" in the tip makes it harder to know when the rifle is going to fire. For this reason, narrow triggers that fit into the index joint are better than wide ones that don't.

WEIGHTY MATTERS What about weight? Noting that the trigger on a Jarrett Signature rifle was set at 1½ pounds, a reader once asked if that was a good pull weight for hunting rifles in general. To which I replied, "Great gobs of goose grease, no!" That Jarrett is a specialty gun. For general use, anything below 3 pounds is asking for it.

If you're excited, or your hands are cold, or you're wearing gloves, or any combination thereof, a trigger pull of less than 3 pounds is going to get you into trouble eventually—the rifle will go off before you're ready. Good dangerous-game rifles have their triggers set at 4 to 5 pounds, and I've pulled some heavier than that.

LIGHTENING UP If you must have a light pull, there are some excellent aftermarket triggers that will hold at a weight of as little as 2 ounces, but you had better practice with them, because controlling a trigger that light takes some thought and effort.

34 CARE FOR YOUR TRIGGER

A trigger has two natural enemies—water and oil. It can rust if it's left wet for days on end, and it will clog if you hose it down with lubricant. There's an easy solution to both problems. If your rifle has been soaked repeatedly, take out the bolt and pump a few squirts of lighter fluid into the trigger so it runs down and out through the mechanism. That heads off corrosion pretty effectively. Before each hunting season begins, take the barreled action out of the stock and give the whole trigger mechanism a good hosing with lighter fluid. That will clean it out thoroughly.

If your trigger gums up due to cold weather, there are a couple of cures. Take the barreled action out of the stock and then pour either Coleman lantern fuel or boiling water through the trigger. That should clear up whatever gunk is stuck in there jamming it.

And remember, no trigger stays adjusted forever. Eventually, they'll all need to be tuned up. If yours starts to drag, creep, or otherwise misbehave, it's off to the gunsmith you go. If a friend says he can tune up your trigger for you, and he's not a gunsmith, get a new friend.

35 AVOID TROUBLE

The first rule of buying used guns is to only buy from dealers who will back what they sell you or from individuals whom you know and trust. Unless you are a firearms expert, don't buy from the guy with the table at the gun show. Tomorrow, he'll be down the road with your money, and you'll be at the gunsmith, fixing up the crummy rifle he sold you. In addition, you should avoid the following:

• Any rifle that shows signs of obvious abuse and neglect: rust, a battered stock, or big patches of bluing worn off. No matter what the price is, just leave it be.

• Any rifle that shows signs of home gunsmithing. There are two kinds of people who work on rifles—those who know how and morons. Amateur tinkering can not only render a rifle useless, but can also make it downright dangerous.

• Any rifle with a rusted bore or chamber. There is no way that gun is going to shoot well, and the least you are looking at is a rebarreling job.

• Bargains that seem too good to be true. If someone offers you a rifle for a fraction of what the gun is really worth, he may be genuinely desperate for quick cash, or he may be trying to sell you a stolen gun. As a rule, if you find a rifle in good condition that is selling for less than a third of its new price, it should be looked at with suspicion.

• Rifles chambered for some kind of obscure wildcat cartridge—or famous wildcat cartridge. Unless you are an advanced handloader, you'll have serious problems getting ammunition, and you'll find it almost impossible to dump the thing when it aggravates you terminally.

36 TELL THE DEALS FROM THE LEMONS

RULE ONE If the rifle is in poor condition, forget about it. The only reason to buy a clunker is for parts.

RULE TWO If you buy a rifle sight unseen, insist on a trial period, during which you can send it back and get a refund if the rifle is not satisfactory.

RULE THREE Many used rifles are sold on consignment, and the prices are not unchangeable once they've gathered dust. That's when you leap up with your checkbook in hand.

RULE FOUR A high price is no guarantee that a rifle will not have problems.

RULE FIVE Beware of dirty rifles. A bore that is fouled with copper is often pitted beneath it, and when you clean the stuff out, you'll probably find that you need to get a new barrel.

RULE SIX Some restoration work can get you a hell of a bargain. See if the seller will allow you to take it to a gunsmith to get an estimate on what it would cost to restore the gun. You may be surprised at how little it will cost you.

37 SPOT THE TOP 10 DEAL BREAKERS

ONE A dirty bore, or a bore with copper streaks. Who knows what lies beneath?

TWO Chips or dings at the muzzle. They ruin accuracy, and the barrel will have to be recrowned.

THREE Rust, anywhere, in any amount at all. This is inexcusable.

FOUR Cracks in the stock.

FIVE Pits in the bolt face. These are a result of blown primers, which means that someone was using the rifle to fire injudicious handloads.

SIX A rifle that fires when the bolt is slammed forward and down. There's not enough sear engagement, which is just plain dangerous.

SEVEN A trigger that is heavy, creepy, or light, or shows signs of having been tampered with.

EIGHT A rifle that will fire when you cock it, put it on safe, pull the trigger, and then throw the safety to the off position.

NINE A chamber that is worn out of round. This comes from the poor use of a cleaning rod and means the rifle will not shoot accurately.

TEN Rifling that's scorched toward the rear of the barrel. This is a sign that the gun is near the end of its useful life.

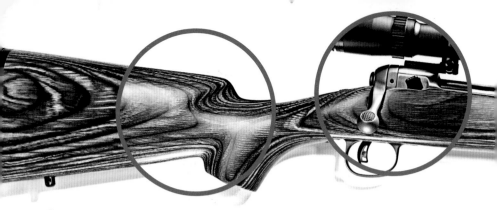

38 DON'T BE AN IDIOT

You're spending a lot of money on this custom gun. Don't blow it. These rules will help you achieve that goal and get the gun you want, whether you know it right now or not.

ESCHEW THE ODD Several years back, Abercrombie & Fitch had a highly engraved used bull-barreled varmint rifle for sale. I think it was in their New York City store for 10 years, and I don't know if it ever did sell. Simply, no one wanted an engraved varmint rifle. Should the sad day come when you must part with your custom gun, and the gun is too strange, you will be unable to recoup any of your investment, at least not within a decade.

BEWARE OF REVOLUTIONARY IDEAS A few years ago, it was trendy to make barrels by wrapping fiberglass thread around a thin steel liner. All sorts of advantages were claimed until someone pointed out that if you put a nick in the fiberglass, the barrel would probably disintegrate. Most other radical attempts at improvement vanish just as quickly.

GET LESS POWER If you think that you need a .300 Magnum of one kind or another, get a .30/06 instead. Convinced you need a 7mm Magnum? Get a .280 or .270. For a deer rifle, you should be thinking of a 7mm/08, .260 Remington, or 6.5x55 Swede. The less the recoil, the better you shoot, and the better you shoot, the more game you get.

PICK A SANE CARTRIDGE It is a given among custom-rifle builders that the clients with the most smarts pick the dullest, oldest cartridges: 7x57 Mauser, .30/06, .270, .375 H&H, and so on. That's because these rounds have been around longer than dirt and have proven themselves through many generations. They won't fail you, either. There are good reasons why few people build rifles for the .30/416 Eargesplitten Loudenboomer.

DON'T GET NUTS ABOUT ACCURACY Any big-game rifle that will shoot a minute of angle will kill anything you aim it at. A half-minute rifle won't make the beasts any deader. In all probability the gun you end up with will shoot better than you can hold. What you're looking for is consistency above everything else. You want all your shots going to the same place all the time.

GET TO KNOW YOUR GUN The best rifle in the world will not transform a poor shot into a decent one or a mediocre shot into a good one. When you get your new rifle, burn some ammo.

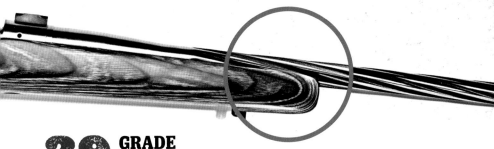

39 GRADE THAT GUN

If you are looking to buy a used gun, the first thing you need to know is that they fit into one of six categories, depending on their condition.

POOR The gun is pitted and rusted, may not be in working order, and may not be safe to shoot. Forget it.

FAIR It works and is safe to shoot, but it has taken a beating. Consider it only if it's dirt cheap and you don't mind paying to have it touched up, or if you want to do the refinishing yourself, or if you just want something you can knock around.

GOOD This gun is in fine working order, but repairs or replacement parts may be needed. It should have around 80 percent of its original finish.

VERY GOOD The gun should have more than 90 percent of its original finish, be in perfect working order, have none of its parts replaced, and need only very small repairs, if any.

EXCELLENT This means that it's just short of brand-new, showing only the most minor signs of wear and use.

NIB (NEW IN BOX) You're looking at a firearm just as it came from the factory, with all the tags, stickers, labels, and everything else. This category is meant more for collectors than shooters.

PETZAL ON: GETTING THE BEST BARGAIN

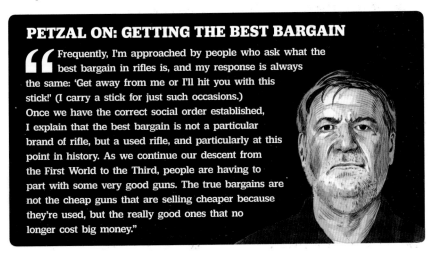

" Frequently, I'm approached by people who ask what the best bargain in rifles is, and my response is always the same: 'Get away from me or I'll hit you with this stick!' (I carry a stick for just such occasions.) Once we have the correct social order established, I explain that the best bargain is not a particular brand of rifle, but a used rifle, and particularly at this point in history. As we continue our descent from the First World to the Third, people are having to part with some very good guns. The true bargains are not the cheap guns that are selling cheaper because they're used, but the really good ones that no longer cost big money."

4⃝ KNOW WHY THAT RIFLE'S FOR SALE

It's natural to think that people trade in rifles because there's something wrong with the gun. Usually that's not actually the case; instead they've likely gone on the used-gun market for one of the following reasons.

IT KICKS Owner falls for ad copy, buys gun, shoots it once, and trades it in for something that kicks less.

DEATH Gun owner takes dirt nap. Kids are not interested in shooting, so the guns go up for sale.

BOREDOM Owner loses interest in shooting for some reason.

IDIOCY Owner trades rifle to get something a gun writer wrote about (worst of all reasons to trade rifle).

POVERTY Owner gets into financial trouble; guns go to raise money.

MOVING Owner moves to new locale where guns are not welcome. Has to get rid of guns before relocating.

DIVORCE Husband and wife go to court. Judge hears both sides. Judge says, "Give her everything." Gun collection goes to pay settlement.

Smith & Wesson Model M&P15 Carbine

PETZAL ON: ARS

" Because the AR is considered by some to be an assault weapon, whatever the hell that is, there are special laws and regulations governing it. In New York State, for example, you can't have an AR magazine that holds more than 10 rounds, and you can't have a muzzle brake. Does this make sense? Of course not, but then neither do most firearms laws."

41 MEET THE MODERN SPORTING RIFLE

The AR (for AR-15, its original model designation) was first issued by the US Army late in 1964 as the M-16 and has gone on to serve longer than any other weapon as our standard infantry rifle. It was a truly radical gun in terms of its weight, construction, and the small-bore high-velocity cartridge it uses.

Despite its military success, it made only very slow inroads with civilian shooters, but around the turn of the 21st century, people who didn't wear uniforms discovered that the AR (or Modern Sporting Rifle, or MSR) was something unique.

TRULY MODULAR The AR can be disassembled and reassembled with ease and reconfigured with all manner of accessories to do all sorts of things. No skill is required, and few tools. It's our first shape-shifting rifle. Because the AR is modular, you can swap out triggers and sights (telescopic, red dot, laser, and iron and mount them in any position you want thanks to the gun's Picatinny Rail bases), swap magazines, change buttstocks and fore-ends, and install a vertical fore-end grip, which makes eminent ergonomic sense. You can shift from one cartridge to another with minimal trouble.

A SOFT KICKER The cartridges the AR uses are light-recoiling to begin with, and unlike older rifle designs, the ARs kick straight back, shifting the jolt from your head, where you can't take it, to your shoulder, where you can. Its gas-operation system and spring-loaded bolt buffer drain off even more kick.

LOTS OF CHEAP AMMO This enables you to shoot for fun. Do know, however, that because MSRs are chambered for small cartridges (.223—or its military version, the 5.56mm—and .308 are by far the most common), you can't hunt everything on the continent with them, although you can certainly hunt a great many species.

HIGHLY DURABLE This one should be fairly obvious. It's a military arm, for heaven's sake.

42 SHOOT ON THE RANGE

A few words of caution: An MSR basically encourages you to shoot as fast as you possibly can and ignore the fact that a rifle is a device for delivering aimed fire. But this gun's virtue lies in its ability to make multiple *aimed* shots easy, not to see how fast you can pop off 10 or 20 rounds.

Also, recall that unlike civilian firearms, for which you can control the cartridge ejection to a degree, the AR sends its empties flying. That hot brass really sails through the air, and if it hits the shooting bench or goes down the neck of the guy next to you, he may not take it in good humor.

Finally, remember that your rifle is a self-loader, and every time you pull the trigger it's going to shove another round in the chamber unless the magazine is empty or you lock the bolt back. Pay attention!

43 CHOOSE AMMO WISELY

AR chambers come in three varieties. Military chambers will handle just about any kind of 5.56mm ammo you want to stuff in them because their tolerances are very generous. However, they don't produce the best accuracy. Match chambers give the best accuracy but will probably not accept some kinds of ammo. The best compromise is a Wylde chamber, which was designed by a gunsmith of the same name and will do a good job with either type of ammunition.

Military ball ammo is cheap but tends to ricochet and can't be humanely used for hunting. Tracer is fun to shoot but will get you thrown off some rifle ranges because it starts fires. Lots of excellent civilian ammo exists for match shooting, varmint hunting, big-game hunting, and target practice, and I would stick to that.

44 GET OUT OF A JAM

Every once in a while, especially when shooting large volumes of ammo or during rapid-fire shooting, you'll get a jam with your AR, and you need to clear it correctly and safely. Here's how.

When you first experience a malfunction, use the simple steps of the **SPORTS** method.

SLAP the bottom of the magazine. This ensures it is seated fully and correctly in the receiver.

PULL the charging handle completely to the rear and hold it there. The bolt should move all the way back and expose the chamber.

OBSERVE the ejection port. See if pulling the charging handle ejected a live round or a spent cartridge that was holding up the works.

RELEASE the charging handle. If the jam has been cleared, this will fully lock the bolt forward and load a new round.

TAP the forward assist. This will help ensure the bolt is fully locked. Once the bolt is locked, pull the charging handle back slightly and do a brass check, ensuring a new round has been seated. Release it and allow it to snap closed fully. Remember to always keep the muzzle of the rifle pointed downrange.

SQUEEZE the trigger. Take aim and attempt to fire a shot.

If that doesn't clear it, or if the charging handle can't be manipulated, you have a more serious jam, and it's time to enlist the help of a gunsmith who can fix the problem for you.

45 BE SAFE WHEN CLEARING JAMS

Jams are a possibility with any type of rifle but seem to occur more often in ARs. The directions that come with your AR will tell you how to clear a stuck case or live round, but there is one overriding principle to the business: Before you start working on the gun, make sure the rifle is pointed in a direction where the bullet will be stopped immediately if the gun goes off.

Keep the rifle level and point the muzzle at a backstop or a dirt bank or whatever else is safe and in plain view. A rifle bullet can travel 3 miles or more with the muzzle elevated 45 degrees and take a life at the end of its journey.

Be careful about pounding on a stuck live round from the muzzle with a cleaning rod. There are two cases on record of this being done in a way that in turn caused the powder charges to detonate, which propelled the cases from the chamber with such force that they killed people standing behind the rifles. Tap on the bullets very gently, and if you are even the slightest bit in doubt, lock the action open and take the thing to a gunsmith.

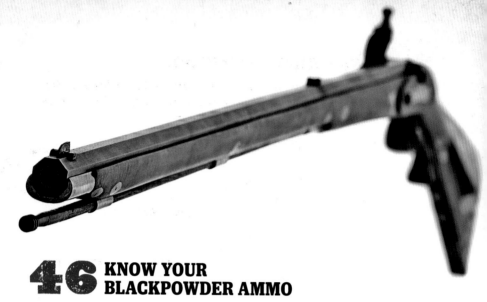

46 KNOW YOUR BLACKPOWDER AMMO

Here's a rundown of the most popular types of bullets used with muzzleloaders. Go with .54, .50, or .45 caliber for big game; .40, .36, and .32 are for small game.

PATCHED ROUND BALL On paper, the round ball's ballistics are pathetic, but it kills far better than it should at ranges inside 100 yards. The cloth patch seals the bore and engages the rifling. In general, round balls shoot best from traditional-style rifles with a slow rate of rifling twist, about one turn in 60 inches.

CONICAL BULLET About twice the weight of the same caliber round ball, a conical bullet hits much harder, shoots flatter, and loads easier. The Thompson/ Center's Maxi-Ball was the first example made for modern hunters. Conicals shoot best from a fast-twist barrel.

SABOTED BULLETS The plastic sabot lets you shoot a slightly smaller bullet from a big-bore gun, resulting in higher velocities. Best of all, good-quality copper-jacketed hunting bullets can be united with sabots, thus putting their penetration and expansion on a par—or very nearly so—with that of centerfire rifle bullets.

POWERBELT Halfway between a conical and a saboted bullet, the PowerBelt is a full-bore projectile with a plastic base that expands to seal the bore, then pops off in flight. Unlike many saboted bullets, PowerBelts slide easily down a rifle's bore for fast loading.

Patched Round Ball

Conical Bullet

Saboted Bullets

PowerBelts

47 KEEP YOUR POWDER DRY

There's a reason this catchphrase is used even by people who have only the foggiest idea what it means. Keeping your powder dry is essential, as a damp charge will not ignite or will behave unpredictably. Here are four handy hints.

TAPE IT UP Put a piece of tape over the muzzle on days when it's raining or snowing.

MAKE IT YOUR BEESWAX After capping your rifle, press beeswax around the bottom edges of the cap to keep moisture out.

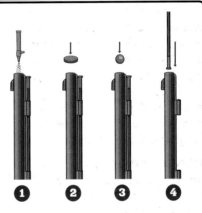

BAG IT Keep your capper in a Ziploc bag.

KEEP IT COLD If you come in for lunch on a cold day, go ahead and leave the gun outside so moisture doesn't condense in the barrel and dampen the charge.

48
LOAD YOUR BLACKPOWDER RIFLE

STEP ONE Pour the powder down the barrel from a powder-measuring tool, which will ensure the correct charge. If you're using pelletized powder, just drop in the proper number.

STEP TWO Load the bullet. For a round ball, lay a patch over the bore and shove the ball down on it. You'll need a ball starter to get it going. A little lube helps; at the range, spit is all you need. In the field, use Crisco or a commercial lubricant. Conicals and PowerBelts go down fairly easily. Sabots can be hard to get down. A little lube helps here, too.

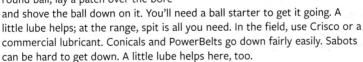

STEP THREE Push the bullet in and tamp it down firmly but carefully with a ramrod. Afterward, leave the ramrod in and scratch a mark on it to show the proper seating depth. You can also use that mark to determine whether or not the rifle has been loaded yet.

STEP FOUR Put on a primer cap if your blackpowder rifle is the percussion type, or fill the pan with powder if it's a flintlock. Remember to take out the ramrod before you even think about pulling the trigger; the only thing you should be firing is the bullet.

49 DECONSTRUCT A CARTRIDGE

1. BULLET The construction of the projectile has a major influence on the effectiveness of the cartridge.

2. NECK Holds the bullet in place and aligns it with the rifling.

3. SHOULDER Modern cases have sharper shoulders–30 degrees or more–than older ones. It's thought that this gives a cleaner, more efficient burn to the powder.

4. CASE A brass or steel shell for the bullet, powder, and primer.

5. POWDER It can be either spherical (ball) or extruded (log) and ranges in burn rate from fast to slow, depending on factors such as the bullet weight, case capacity, and shape of the case.

6. TAPER Modern cases have very little body taper; older ones have a lot. Low taper makes room for more powder, but more taper means more reliable feed.

7. RIM Rimless cases have rims that barely extend beyond the extraction groove. By contrast, rimmed cases lack the groove and have wider rims.

8. BASE The base of the case carries the primer pocket and the headstamp, which designates caliber and make.

9. PRIMER Composed of a cup, anvil, and a small charge of explosive compound. Primers come in several sizes, and there are some with longer-burning flames, for Magnum charges of slow powder.

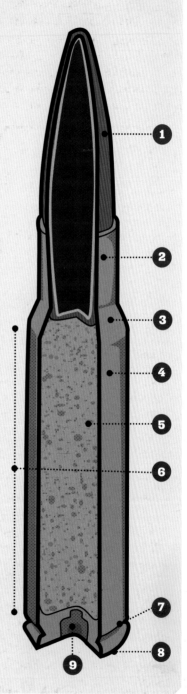

50 UNDERSTAND WHY THESE ROUNDS RULE

I promised you the ugly truth, and one of the ugliest facts is this: Choice of cartridge ranks fairly low in determining whether you will succeed as a hunter. If you're a good shot, it doesn't matter much what you use. On the other hand, choosing the wrong round can screw you up royally. With that contradiction firmly in mind, here are my top choices in each category, and why I chose them.

SMALL GAME

.22 Long Rifle This gun has no recoil, a comparatively mild report, extraordinary accuracy, and an essential lack of destructive force, which is just what the job calls for. You can choose between regular velocity, high velocity, and hypervelocity, and between solid-point and hollow-point ammo. I rule out hypervelocity (too destructive and not accurate enough), which leaves regular or high velocity, both of which are fine. I prefer hollow points over solids because they're more certain killers.

Favorite Load Winchester High-Speed Hollow Points

VARMINTS

.223 Remington Known to the military as the 5.56mm, this hugely popular cartridge shoots a 50-grain bullet at 3,300 fps muzzle velocity. When being considered as a military round, it has its detractors, but for varmints (which these days basically means prarie dogs), it is a standout. Among its virtues is low recoil, which is very important because your sight picture must not be disturbed. It also heats up barrels far less than larger .22 centerfires, it's as accurate as anything out there, and, as an extra bonus, there's tons of cheap .223 ammo around.

Favorite Load Winchester 50-grain Ballistic Silvertip

VARMINTS AND BIG GAME

6mm Remington Through no fault of its own, the 6mm is less popular than the .243, but it's still a better cartridge. I used both of them for years and found I could always get better velocities with the 6mm. The best factory bullet for varmints is the 80-grain at a listed 3,500 fps; for deer, the 100-grain at 3,100. (In the typical 22-inch-barreled 6mm, you'll find these figures to be wildly optimistic.) Fifteen years ago, I'd have told you that the 6mm is an uncertain killer on big game because the bullets are just too small; however, bullets are now so much better that the objection is withdrawn.

Favorite Load Remington 100-grain Core-Lokt

BIG GAME: THE LIGHT KICKERS

7x57 Mauser and 7mm/08 Remington Why did I choose two? Because even though one of them is very old (the 7x57) another is comparatively modern, ballistically they are alike as peas in a pod (140- or 150-grain bullets at 2,700 fps, give or take a couple of feet). Lots of 7mm/08 rifles are around, and tons of 7x57s. Here is what these cartridges will not do: knock you sideways with recoil or deafen you with muzzle blast. If you wish to use them in short, light rifles, you may do so and the recoil will not cause your lamentations to reach unto heaven. Here is what they will do: kill most species of big game within any reasonable range. Right now. Dead.

Favorite Loads 7x57 Federal Power-Shok 140-grain and Speer Hot-Cor SP 7mm/08 Winchester Supreme 140-grain Ballistic Silvertip

BIG GAME: THE ALL-AROUND ROUNDS

.30/06 Springfield You thought I was going to pick something else and get drummed out of the Gun Writers' Guild and spend the rest of my life being hunted like a criminal? Fat chance. Nope, sorry. The '06 is the unquestioned champ in the do-everything category. Now in its 101st year, the '06 is loaded with bullets ranging in weight from 125 grains to 220 grains, but of these, the most useful are 150 grains at 2,900 fps, 165 grains at 2,800, and 180 grains at 2,700. And you can find all sorts of inexpensive military ammo floating around. Among handloaders, it is no secret that with caution and slow-burning powder, factory ballistics can be significantly bettered. Handloaders also know that one of the most useful bullets for the '06 is the 200-grain slug, which is not available from the factories.

Favorite Loads Of the endless variety out there, I'll try to narrow it down to two: Federal Premium Vital-Shok with the 150-grain Nosler Ballistic Tip (shown) and the same brand with the 180-grain Barnes TSX

BIG GAME AT LONG RANGE

.300 Weatherby Magnum Let me be the first to acknowledge the various huge .30s made by Remington, Lazzeroni, and Dakota, all of which will do everything this one will do, but the Weatherby got here first, and its track record on game is equaled by few other cartridges. If you'd like to kill something, especially a big something, far, far away, use this. Weatherby loads the .300 with bullets ranging in weight from 150 grains (at 3,500 fps) to 220 (at 2,850). But there are only two weights you should consider: the 180-grain at 3,150, or the 200 at 3,000 or just a bit under. The heavier slugs carry just as well as light ones, fight the wind better, and do not result in a lot of ruined meat. Recoil and muzzle blast are for experienced shooters only. Take that to heart.

Favorite Loads
Weatherby 180- or 200-grain Nosler Partition

HEAVY OR DANGEROUS NORTH AMERICAN GAME

.338 Winchester Magnum Despite its serious recoil, this thumper is highly popular because it's amazingly versatile. With 200- or 210-grain bullets (which travel around 2,900 fps), it is a terrific long-range round that will make the deer drop. With 225- to 250-grain slugs, it will handle really large critters with aplomb. A strong 250-grain .338 slug gives tremendous straight-line penetration that you do not get from anything else. You wanna break an elk's shoulder? Here's your cartridge. Recoil is stiff; if your .338 weighs less than 9 pounds with scope, you will regret it.

Favorite Load
Remington Premier 225-grain Swift A-Frame

51 KNOW YOUR GAME BULLET OPTIONS

Game bullets come in three types: varmint, deer, and controlled-expanding.

VARMINT BULLETS are very accurate and very fragile. They're intended to do a maximum amount of damage and not ricochet. This is achieved through the use of a hollow point, very thin copper jacket, and soft lead core.

DEER BULLETS are built so they combine a reasonable amount of penetration with rapid expansion, and all of them use some or all of these elements: a lead core, copper-alloy jacket that is thin at the nose and thick at the base, "skiving" (grooves cut into the jacket's interior to ensure rapid expansion) and—in the better ones—a jacket that is chemically bonded to the core to ensure that the bullet holds together when fired.

CONTROLLED-EXPANDING BULLETS give modest expansion while retaining nearly all of their weight, even when fired into thick hide and heavy bones and muscles. Where a deer bullet might retain 50 percent of its weight after striking an animal, a controlled-expansion slug will keep 90 percent plus, and this greater mass ensures it will penetrate nearly anything. Controlled-expansion bullets come in two types—conventional, which employ lead cores and heavy, bonded copper jackets, and the newer variety, which are all copper or copper alloy. These bullets, although quite expensive (copper costs a lot more than lead), are extremely effective and, very often, exceedingly accurate.

Varmint Bullet

Deer Bullet

52 IDENTIFY BULLET SHAPES

SPITZER A pointed bullet, more streamlined than a round-nose, but structurally less strong. All bullets designed for use at long range are spitzers, as are all military bullets.

ROUND-NOSE A bullet with a blunt nose. Round-noses are employed on dangerous-game bullets and on bullets that are used in rifles with tubular magazines, where a spitzer point could detonate the primer of the cartridge ahead of it.

SEMI-SPITZER A shape that falls somewhere in between and combines the advantages and disadvantages of both types.

FLAT-BASE A bullet with no taper at its base. Not aerodynamic, but strong.

Flat-based
Spitzer

Flat-based
Round-nose

Boattail Spitzer

VLD

BOATTAIL A bullet whose base tapers toward the bottom, like a boat's stern when viewed from above. Boattails and spitzer points are usually combined.

REBATED BOATTAIL A boattail that curves inward, leading to a base that is of markedly smaller diameter than that of the bullet. It's more streamlined than a simple boattail.

VLD Very Low Drag is the most extreme type of bullet streamlining, incorporating a very sharp point with a long taper and a rebated boattail.

Conventional Controlled-Expanding Bullet

All-Copper Controlled-Expanding Bullet

53 FORGET ABOUT HYPERVELOCITY

With every decade, cartridges get bigger and muzzle velocities get higher. Maybe it's time to ask why. Now it's true that you can kill a tiger with a .250/3000, or with a .22 Long Rifle (and I will come to visit you in prison), but it is a stunt. High velocity by itself does not kill anything faster than standard velocity. I started out believing devoutly in speed and more speed, but 40 years later, having shot creatures of all sizes with just about everything that goes bang, I've never been able to find any correlation between bullet speed and sudden animal demise. For 15 years, I hunted whitetails in South Carolina, where you can shoot lots and lots of deer, so I had the opportunity to draw some valid comparisons. The smallest cartridge I used was the .257 Roberts; in other years I used the .270 Winchester, .257 Weatherby, and 7mm Weatherby. None of these rounds killed anything any faster or deader than any other cartridge. The same was true with the .338, .340 Weatherby, and .338 Remington Ultra Magnum, all of which I have used a lot. The latter two give anywhere from 250 to 300 fps more than the former, which is a bunch, but the beasts do not go down any quicker. In addition, consider the following.

RECOIL A high-velocity-loaded rifle can generate 28 to 40 foot-pounds of recoil, which is tolerable only to experienced shooters and the criminally insane. In addition, muzzle blast also rises in proportion to velocity.

IMPACT When you get bullets traveling at 3,000 fps and more (sometimes way more), even the strongest and slowest-expanding of them makes a mess of whatever it hits unless the shot is long enough to let some of the velocity drain off. If you are a trophy hunter and don't mind an acre or so of hamburger around the entrance hole, this is not an objection. But if you like wild meat and are disturbed by the waste of same, it is a problem.

BARREL LIFE It's considerably shorter for the super-speed than it is for standard-velocity loads. A well-cared-for .30/06 (60 grains of powder per cartridge) will give you about 5,000 rounds of first-class accuracy. Any of the super .30s (80 grains of powder) will get perhaps 1,500 before they start to deteriorate. This gets expensive fast.

54 REMEMBER BILLY DIXON

In the 1870s, at a place called Adobe Walls in Texas, a group of buffalo hunters was trapped in an abandoned mission by a band of Comanche warriors who looked forward to slitting them from crotch to brisket with a dull deer antler. Things looked bad for the hunters until one Billy Dixon shot the Comanche leader dead at what was probably close to a mile, and the rest of the war party remembered they had pressing business elsewhere. Dixon made this shot with a .50 Sharps buffalo rifle, which hurled a lumbering 500-grain bullet at roughly 1,200 fps. Instead of a scope, he had a peep sight called a vernier sight. Rangefinder? Nope. Ballistics program? Nope. Shooting experience? Plenty. Incentive? Loads. It worked for him, and it can work for you.

55 DO HIGH VELOCITY RIGHT

Why does high velocity keep getting higher, and horrific super loads keep appearing? Because nothing makes hitting at long distances easier than a good dose of feet per second. If you think you will ever need to take a shot at 300 yards and more, high velocity is your very best friend.

However, it's also the case that speed alone will not solve all your problems in hitting at long range. You also need resistance to wind drift and momentum, or the ability to sustain velocity way out there. The way you get it is by going not to light bullets that give the highest initial velocity, but making use of the heavier slugs in a given caliber, and bullets that are streamlined.

For example, if you have a 7mm Magnum, you want 160-grain bullets in preference to 140- or 150-grain. If your rifle is one of the real 7mm monsters, you may find that 175-grainers are the way to go. In .30 caliber, look for nothing lighter than 180-grain, and so on. As for bullets, you want sharp points (preferably polycarbonate) and boattails, both of which increase a slug's ballistic coefficient.

The truth about high velocity is that it is a mixed blessing. But when your target is a dot in the distance, it is the deadliest thing since cholera.

56 SHOOT MORE, SHOOT BETTER

In 1965, I worked up my first handload, took myself to the range, and sat cowering behind the rifle for five minutes before I worked up the nerve to pull the trigger. I was convinced that I was about to splatter important parts of my person up and down the firing line. Many thousands of handloads later, I'm still intact. I've also ended up saving a ton of money, become a better rifle shot, and gotten superior accuracy from legions of rifles.

I know a number of very good rifle shots, and without exception, they load their own ammo. The reason for this is that if you want to shoot well, you have to shoot a lot. The only way you can afford to shoot a lot is to make a lot of money or load your own ammo. I've found that it's a lot easier to load your own ammo.

The most expensive component in a round of centerfire ammunition is the brass case—just under 50 percent of the total cost, in fact—and if you can save that case and substitute your labor for the factory's in loading it, you can suddenly afford to shoot in volume. Once you buy your basic tools—press, scale, dies, primer seater, et cetera—you're pretty much done, because nothing wears out.

Your only expense over the long term is the components, which is to say powder, bullets, primers, and cases. (Yes, the cases do wear out eventually, but unless your pressures are high, you can get 10 to 15 loadings out of a brass case without much trouble.) Look for bargains. Someone is always having a sale or going out of business, and that is when you jump in.

In addition, there's the fact that only the handloader knows the joy of switching to a different powder, or using a half grain more or less, or changing primer brands, or seating the bullet a little farther in or a little farther out, and seeing mediocre groups turn into bragging groups. It's magic, is what it is.

57 LOAD YOUR OWN AMMO

Getting started requires less money than you'd think, and the equipment never wears out. (I'm still using a lot of the gear that I bought in the mid '60s.) You will need: a press, a powder measure, a die set, a powder trickler, a caliper to measure case lengths, a case trimmer, a deburring tool, a primer pocket cleaner, case lube, a powder scale, a powder funnel, and a loading manual. That's the basic gear list. If it all seems like too much to keep track of, you can buy a starter kit that will have almost everything you need.

Loading your own ammo is not as hard as you'd think. It requires no mechanical aptitude and no manual dexterity.

It's a series of very simple steps. The exact details vary depending on the ammo in question, which is why you need to get a couple of loading manuals and read them before you even start. You will then have a grasp of the basics. What the manuals can't supply is judgment—how to gauge pressures, how to look at a group that's not so tight and be able to tighten it. This is something you get from experience and from consulting with other handloaders who know what they're talking about.

All of that said, here are the very basic steps.

1. Clean inside the case's neck with a bristle brush.

2. Lubricate the case lightly on the lube pad.

3. Run the case through the sizing die using your bullet press; this will also remove any used primer.

4. Check your case's length with the caliper. Trim the case with the trimmer if needed.

5. Use your deburring tool to smooth the inside and outside of the case's mouth.

6. Clean the primer pocket with your primer pocket brush.

7. Prime the case using your priming tool.

8. Weigh out the powder on your scale and pour it into the case using a powder funnel.

9. Seat the bullet into the case using the bullet seating die.

 **KEEP IT SAFE**

Handloading is considerably safer than driving. When you're making your own ammunition, you don't have to share the road with homicidal maniacs texting away at 70 mph. What the hobby does require is that you understand what you're doing, do not assume that you know more than the loading manuals, and pay attention. I feel a lot easier about smokeless powder in my house than I do about gasoline cans in the garage. Primers are very stable; all they ask is that you handle them with the respect they deserve. It's unwise and unnecessary to keep a lot of powder on hand. Although smokeless powder may be no more dangerous than cleaning fluid or propane or gasoline, you don't want a ton of it in your house because if you do have

a fire and it catches, you will have a really dandy blaze to contend with. On top of that, there may be legal restrictions on how much you can store inside a residential dwelling, so be sure to check. Then keep only what you need on hand, and no more. And if you have kids around, keep all your reloading gear (including primers and powder) locked up.

 **SHUN CHEAP BINOCULARS**

Cheap binoculars are worse than no binoculars. You need to spend a little money, but bargains are out there. Go cheaper than a few hundred bucks, and you are likely to end up with an inanimate hideosity. I've never known someone to spend money on good binoculars and regret it. The usual reaction is, "Why did I wait so long?"

59   FUNDAMENTALS
GET GOOD GLASS

Along with your rifle and scope, binoculars are the most important piece of hunting equipment you can own. I've met guides who dressed in rags and lived on wallpaper paste and government cheese but owned a pair of $2,000 binoculars. The reason was simple: Finding game was their livelihood, and nothing did it half so well as the really good glasses. Friends may fail you; your family may stab you in the back; your dog may pee on your leg; but top-line binoculars will never let you down.

COMFORT If you are using a binocular properly, you will look through it by the hour. If your glass is a good one, you will be able to do this with no trouble. But poor-quality binoculars, as my late friend Gary Sitton once said, "will suck the eyeballs out of your skull."

LONGEVITY Top-line binoculars, though they may become technically obsolete because they lack some sensational new feature, will still be top-line binoculars long after you have fired your last shot.

VALUE People who just have to have the latest and most advanced of everything will trade off a pair of first-rate binoculars quicker than you can say "exit pupil." For this reason, there are spectacular deals online and at gun shows for used top-line glass.

61 SPEAK FLUENT BINOCULAR

LENSES AND PRISMS A lens brings an object into focus. But when you look at an object through a lens, it appears upside down, and you need to put the image right side up before it reaches your eye. That's the job of the prism, a wedge-shaped assemblage of glass pieces that bends the light coming through a lens. There are two types: roof and porro. Roof-prism binoculars demand greater precision in manufacture than porros and are usually more expensive. But most hunters choose them anyway because they are more compact than porro-prism models. Lenses are often used in combination to cancel out each other's optical faults. A lens that is alone is called a singlet, two lenses used together is a doublet, three is a triplet.

POWER Another term for magnification, 'power' is almost always expressed along with the size of the objective lenses in millimeters. Therefore, a 7x35 glass magnifies seven times, and its objective lenses are 35 millimeters in diameter. The most popular strengths for hunting are 8X and 10X. The lower the power, the wider your field of view and the easier it is to hold the binocular steady. Still, I have always preferred 10X glasses. The field of view shrinks, and it's harder to hold them steady, but you get to see in detail. I own two pairs of binoculars in 12X that I have used for elk hunting and varmint hunting, and I love them madly.

BRIGHTNESS The objective-lens diameter determines the amount of light that enters the glass. The bigger they are in relation to magnification, the brighter the glass (in theory at least). A 7x42 binocular will be brighter than a 7x35 because of the larger objective. The other number you need to know when thinking about brightness is the diameter of the exit pupil. All else being equal, the bigger the brighter. The way you calculate the size of the exit pupil is done by dividing the diameter of the objective lens by the magnification of the instrument. So a 10x42 binocular has an exit pupil of 4.2. The same glass in 8x42 has an exit pupil of 5.3 and will be brighter.

62 KNOW YOUR COATINGS

When light passes through glass, it tends to reflect in all directions. This causes the image to dim, distorts the colors you see, degrades contrast, and may give you leprosy for all I know. The solution is to apply a coat of magnesium fluoride that is .00004 to .00006 inch thick. Much shuck and jive about coatings is foisted on the public. There are four levels involved in this process, which Thomas McIntyre admirably describes in his excellent little book *The Field & Stream Hunting Optics Handbook* as follows.

COATED A single layer of coating has been lavishly slapped on at least one lens surface, somewhere.

FULLY COATED A single layer has been applied to all the "air to glass" surfaces, which includes the two sides of any air-spaced elements inside the optics.

MULTICOATED Several layers of antireflective coating have been applied to at least one lens surface.

FULLY MULTICOATED All air-to-glass surfaces have received multiple layers of antireflective coating.

But we are not yet done with coatings. When light passes through roof prisms, the wavelengths of different colors of the spectrum do so at different rates, and the result is a degraded image. The cure is a process called "phase coating," to correct this issue. All self-respecting roof-prism binoculars are phase-coated.

63 FOLLOW THE LIGHT

Are you not really sure what happens when you peer through a pair of binoculars? Here's a quick overview for you.

Light, and the image it carries, does what it wants, not what you want, so the job of a binocular is to keep it under control. The objective lens [a] gathers the image, simultaneously inverting it, and sending it down the binocular barrel to the focus lens [b], which is set in a housing that moves forward and backward and is in turn controlled by the focus wheel [c].

The image next encounters the roof prism [d], whose job it is to turn the image right side up. (In order to avoid light loss by all this bouncing around, the prism's surfaces are given what is known as phase coating to prevent light dispersion.) This is done by reflecting it from as many as 16 surfaces, until it arrives, exhausted but erect, at the ocular lens [e], which magnifies it.

Duplex-type Reticles

Range-compensating
Reticles

64 SCOPE IT OUT

TUBES Today's rifles scopes are drawn from aircraft-grade aluminum and are available in two finishes: shiny and matte. A shiny scope tube is nothing more than a warning light that says to animals, "Why die when you can run?" A hunter needs a shiny scope tube like he needs a freshly polished tuba.

Tubes come in two diameters—1 inch and 30mm. It's claimed that 30mm tubes allow more light in. I doubt it. But they are structurally stronger and allow more latitude of adjustment, which helps you get your rifle on the paper even if something is out of alignment somewhere.

BELLS At either end of the scope tube are the objective-lens housing, or bell, and the ocular-lens housing, or bell (this is the one that cracks you in the eyebrow). As the power of the scope increases and/or the manufacturer wants to admit more light, the size of the objective bell increases. Most for hunting are between 40mm and 50mm. I'm perfectly happy with 40mm or 42mm most of the time. The bigger the lens, the more the scope weighs, the more it costs, the clumsier it makes the rifle to handle, and the more difficult it is to mount on the receiver.

ADJUSTMENTS All scopes have adjustments for windage (lateral) and elevation (up and down). The elevation dial is at 12 o'clock, the windage dial at 3 o'clock. What these dials are supposed to do, via a system of small, fragile, and treacherous parts, is adjust where you place the crosshairs to match the bullet's point of impact. Most scopes claim to change the point of impact $\frac{1}{4}$ inch per click at 100 yards. In reality, they do what they please, and you just have to live with it. The best windage and elevation adjustments move with a solid, firm click or a thunk, and this is one of the things to look for when you buy a scope. Some scopes also have adjustment for parallax, to adjust the sight-picture's focus at precise distances, which is handy if you'll shoot at long range or at small targets.

The simplest of all adjustments is focus. To focus a scope, point it at the sky or a wall and turn the ocular-lens bell until the reticle appears sharp. Then lock the bell in place. If there's no locking ring, you need to get a better scope.

EYE RELIEF This is the distance between the ocular-lens bell and your eye when

you're looking through it; if you don't have enough of it, you will eventually hear the melodious sound of aluminum splitting your eyebrow. Eye relief decreases in proportion to scope power. Depending on how much your rifle kicks, you need an absolute minimum of 3 inches. On a heavy-kicking rifle, 4 is the least you can get away with.

LENSES The quality of the glass and the coating applied to it determine in large part how good a scope is. Even if you know nothing about scopes, you can look through a $200 scope, and then a $1,200 scope, and know instantly which is which. The difference in image quality is startling, and is what you pay all that money for.

RETICLES In the 1960s, Leupold developed the Duplex crosshair, and that has been the standard for hunters ever since. It pulls your eye to the center, which makes for fast aiming, and also makes it possible to aim with precision. Of all the reticles that are out there, I believe it's the best.

In recent years, manufacturers have added LEDs to their reticles, and here's what I can tell you about them: First, they function extremely well. Second, I'm not quite sure why we even need them.

Range-compensating reticles consist of crosshairs on the vertical stadia wire of the scope that show where to hold for a given distance, sometimes out to 600 yards. They work extremely well provided you read the directions and pay strict attention to them.

65 POWER DOWN (OR UP)

The more power you have, the more difficult it is to keep a steady hold, and the greater the effect that mirage has on your sight picture. Powerful scopes are also bulky, heavy, and expensive. Ultimately, less is more. Today, the variable-power scope is supreme because it offers a degree of flexibility that is genuinely useful. Here's a rough guide to the power ranges that work best.

BIG GAME
3X–9X or 2X–10X

DANGEROUS GAME
1X–4X

VARMINTS
6X–24X

QUICK SHOT

66 SEE THE TARGET

A deer-size animal looks very small at 400 yards; that is why variable-power scopes that magnify up to 10X were invented. Here is what the typical whitetail looks like with the scope cranked to 9X. More magnification means more reticle movement with each twitch.

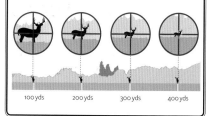

100 yds   200 yds   300 yds   400 yds

67 MARK THE SPOT WITH A DOT

Red-dot sights are optical sights, but unlike scopes they don't magnify, and there's no crosshair—just a red dot. Red dots offer some distinct advantages over scopes: They're smaller, lighter, tougher, and faster to get on target. They have unlimited eye relief, which makes them a natural for a heavy rifle. For a firearm that will be used inside of 200 yards, they deserve very serious consideration.

Their disadvantage is that they don't magnify. So if you have geezer eyesight, or are going to shoot at long range or at small targets, you'll need some Xs in your scope.

68 DIAL IT BACK

Because of the current tactical craze, an increasing number of scopes have exposed dials with no caps over them. I believe these have no place on a big-game rifle. Snipers need them because they routinely crank in windage and elevation adjustments to compensate for the extreme ranges at which they shoot. But because these knobs are exposed, they can turn accidentally, or be damaged by a blow that a capped dial would survive.

69 AVOID FOGGED LENSES

When you hunt in truly cold weather, develop the habit of holding your breath as you raise the rifle to aim. If you don't, you may breathe on your scope's ocular lens, and you'll find yourself trying to aim through a fogbank. You can cloud up even the fog-proof coatings on the newest scopes; they're designed to deal with water droplets, not breath vapor. This applies to binoculars as well.

70 MOUNT IT RIGHT

When mounting a scope, many shooters set it in the rings so that the vertical crosshair tilts right or left. That's because when you rest your cheek on the comb and look through the sight, your head is canted.

The problem with an out-of-kilter vertical crosshair is that it is out of line with the axis of the bore, and thus your bullets will not fly in line with it.

To ensure a straight crosshair, you want to simply put the fore-end of the rifle on a

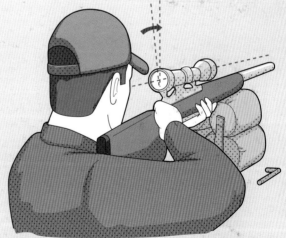

solid rest, then position your head behind the butt of the rifle and sight through the scope. You'll be able to see very clearly whether the crosshair is tilted. If it is, correct accordingly.

71 EXORCISE DEMONS FROM YOUR RIFLE

Rifles do not actually suffer from demonic possession; they only seem to behave that way sometimes. They will not swivel their heads 360 degrees and hurl in your general direction, but they will cause you to miss, which is probably worse. Life's tough enough without inaccurate rifles. Here's how to cure them—and avoid them.

CHECK THE SCOPE In many cases, "inaccurate" rifles are not inaccurate at all but are wearing ruptured scopes. To see if the scope adjustments work, try "squaring the circle." Fire a shot; then, aiming at the same point each time, move the reticle 12 clicks (3 inches) up; then 12 clicks right; then 12 down; then 12 left. You should end up with four shots forming a square. If you don't, then you should send the scope back to the manufacturer for repair.

CLEAN THE BARREL Rifle barrels must have absolutely uniform dimensions (to the ten-thousandth of an inch) for the entire length of their bores in order to be accurate. So when you don't clean a barrel and the copper fouling starts building up, accuracy goes out the window.

SHOOT DIFFERENT AMMO If the gun still won't group the way you'd like, try all the different ammo you can get your hands on because some rifles "prefer" one brand and weight of bullet over another.

SEND IT BACK If you experiment as far as your budget and your patience will let you, and the rifle still won't group, your next step is to send it straight back to the manufacturer.

72 FIGURE OUT YOUR BULLET'S TRAJECTORY

From the instant a bullet leaves the barrel, it begins to drop. How much? The only way to find out for sure is to go out with your rifle and whatever ammo you favor and shoot at 100, 200, and 300 yards. Sight in your rifle to hit 3 inches high at 100. Then, set up a National Rifle Association 50-Yard Slow Fire Pistol Target (the one with the 8-inch-diameter bull) at 200 yards, hold right on the center, and fire five shots. You'll probably see no drop at all. If you do, make a note of it.

Move back to 300 yards and try the same thing. If your rifle produces at least 3,000 fps, you'll probably get a drop of 3 inches below the center of the bull. If you're working with 2,600 to 2,850 fps, then you'll see a drop of 6 to 8 inches from the center.

When the time comes to shoot at something that's alive, you'll have very little to do in the way of calculation. If your bullet drops 3 or 4 inches from center, hold where you normally would, more or less on the center of the body. If the drop is 6 to 8 inches, you may or may not have to allow for it. On a big animal like an elk or a caribou, I would hold a handbreadth (4 inches) high. For a smaller target (an antelope or ratty little whitetail, for example), I'd allow two handbreadths. Whatever you do, as long as you know that the range is no more than 300 yards, never hold out of the hair. Untold numbers of animals have fled from bullets whizzing over their backs.

Hold low when you're shooting uphill or downhill. The closer to vertical a bullet flies—either high or low—the less it drops over distance. How much to hold? I can't tell you. I can only advise that you will probably end up missing more shots due to overcompensating rather than undercompensating.

73 CALCULATE WIND DRIFT

I've seen numerous formulas for calculating wind drift in the field, none of which are any good when your brain is boiling prior to a shot. The only workable one comes from my friend and colleague Wayne van Zwoll. According to Wayne, if you're shooting 180-grain .30/06 bullets at 2,700 fps, and the wind is coming at 10 mph from a right angle, allow 1 inch at 100 yards, 2 inches at 200, 6 inches at 300, and 12 inches at 400. If the wind is coming from 45 degrees instead of 90, you halve these allowances. If it's blowing 20 mph, you double them.

Watch the wind out where the animal is. The wind where you are is not going to have much effect on the bullet. The most important thing is to practice shooting in the wind. A couple of years ago, I was shooting a .308 at 600 yards in South Dakota and being coached by a former member of the Marine Corps rifle team. He was giving me very accurate wind adjustments out of his head, and I asked him how the hell he did it. "Easy," he said. "You watch ten or twenty thousand 7.62 bullets go downrange and you get to know just what the wind will do. If it were another cartridge I wouldn't have a clue."

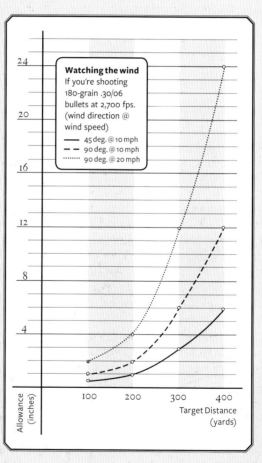

Watching the wind
If you're shooting 180-grain .30/06 bullets at 2,700 fps. (wind direction @ wind speed)

— 45 deg. @ 10 mph
– – 90 deg. @ 10 mph
······· 90 deg. @ 20 mph

Allowance (inches)

Target Distance (yards)

74 GET READY TO GET BETTER

How to improve your shooting? First item on the list is a good .22 rifle, as close as possible to what you use for hunting—not some piece of junk you got at a tag sale, but a serious, accurate firearm. It should be wearing a good scope.

Next comes the ammo. In order to follow the rest of the plan below, you're going to need every bit of accuracy you can muster, so you're obliged to buy at least half a dozen different boxes of ammo (skip the hypervelocity stuff, which I've never seen shoot really well). Get high and standard velocity, both solid and hollow point.

Shoot five-shot groups from a bench at 25 yards with each box. Eventually you will see that one type of ammunition is much more accurate in your rifle than anything else. Get at least a brick of the stuff, which is 500 rounds.

Last on the list are targets. You're after either the NRA 50-Foot Rifle Target (A-36) or the NRA Rifle Silhouettes Target (TQ-14), which are printed by the National Target Company. The former has a dozen bull's-eyes each about the size of a silver dollar. The latter reproduces the four iron targets used on actual silhouette ranges—chickens, wild pigs, turkeys, and rams, five of each to a row.

75 SHOOT, SCORE, AND SHOOT AGAIN

Post your target sheet at 25 yards. The choice of shooting positions is up to you, provided that you dedicate at least half your practice to the offhand position, which is by far the hardest and one that comes up in the field a surprisingly large percentage of the time. You can shoot kneeling, sitting, or any way you please as long as you don't use a rest.

If you're shooting at the bull's-eyes, give yourself five shots at one bull, taking the absolute minimum amount of time to shoulder the rifle, find the bull in the scope, put the crosshairs on it, and fire.

With the silhouette target, take one shot at each little critter in a single row. Your goal in this regimen is speed as much as it is accuracy. Squeeze the trigger no more than five seconds after you have shouldered the rifle.

Score yourself after every five rounds. A hit anywhere in the bull's-eye counts. I find that if I'm really concentrating, 12 bulls (or 12 rows on the silhouette target) is about all I can handle in a session before my mental focus wavers and the crosshairs begin jumping around uncontrollably.

You may find that this drill is less discouraging if you move closer than 25 yards at first, and you may not want to shoot up a whole target.

Over the course of a month or more (or that brick of 500 rounds, whichever you go through first), you should get to the point where you put either four or five hits on every bull on a target. Once you're able to do that, go sight in your centerfire rifle, because you'll be ready for anything the wonderful world of rifle hunting can deal out to you.

76 ASSUME THE POSITION

Tragically, we can't take our benchrests with us into the woods. Still, you can get very steady if you're willing to practice and have the presence of mind to use what's available as support. Here are the positions I've found most useful.

OFFHAND Everyone hates it, nobody practices it, and that's why so many animals escape so many bullets. To shoot offhand, first make sure that your trigger-finger arm **[a]** is more or less parallel to the ground. This forms a pocket for the butt (the rifle's, not yours) and keeps you from placing it out on your arm. This is the old-fashioned method. It's now considered more effective to raise your arm, get the butt into your shoulder, and then let your arm sag down again. Maybe. But the old method looks better, and looking good is as important as shooting good. A sling in the offhand position is worthless. Unless you can get your left arm down on something solid, you get no benefit from it. As for the arm that supports the fore-end **[b]**, keep it directly under the rifle. Or try to. I can't manage it for more than a second or two. My arm invariably wanders off to the side. But if you obey the first principle of offhand shooting, it won't matter. That principle is to shoot fast. I repeat: Shoot fast. You are not going to be able to hold very steady for very long, and the longer you screw around, the worse it's going to get.

PRONE I love prone because I get to lie down and because it's the steadiest position of all. Sadly, you don't often get a shot this way because nature usually puts something between your muzzle and your target. To take advantage of prone, you have to have some kind of support for the rifle in addition to your quivering left arm. (I assume you are one of those degenerates who shoots right-handed.) This can be a sling, a backpack, a rock with your hat on top of it, or, best of all, a bipod. If you're using a sling, your left forearm **[a]** should be directly under the rifle, as close to vertical as you can get it. The sling should be tight enough to turn your left hand blue with red streaks. Purple is also acceptable. Instead of lying flat on the ground with both legs splayed out, bring your right leg **[b]** up toward your chest. This raises your torso and minimizes the effect of your heartbeat and breathing. Finally, avoid a bloody noggin by making sure you have enough eye relief **[c]** because prone gets your forehead closer to the scope than any other position.

SITTING This is the steadiest position after lying prone, but it takes some time to get into and often doesn't get you high enough off the ground. That said, the key to getting it right is to rest the points of your elbows on the flesh of your legs, just behind the knees **[a]**. If the bone of either elbow rests on the bone of either knee, you will wobble. When you're sitting in a tree stand, it's all but impossible to get your knees high enough to use for support. So install a shooting rail or, at the very least, bring a shooting staff.

KNEELING I would like to be buried in the kneeling position. It's very fast to get into. It gets you over most ground cover and is steady if you execute it correctly. Your right butt cheek rests on your right heel **[a]**, and in this case, your left elbow should be thrust past your left knee **[b]** so that your tricep, rather than the point of your elbow, is resting on the knee. I've tried using a sling from the kneeling position, but I don't seem to get any benefit from it. You, on the other hand, may have better luck.

77 AVOID THE LOW BLOW

In rifle shooting, it's axiomatic that the closer you get to the ground, the more accurate you are. But the corollary to that is, the lower you go, the more you get pounded because your body gives less and less with the force of recoil. With a gun that really kicks, it will behoove you to shoot offhand and look for some kind of support rather than use the sitting or (shudder) prone position.

78 HUG A TREE

Shooting offhand is very unsteady, and many hunters tend to stand there and wobble as the agonizing seconds tick by. Instead, head for the nearest tree. Take off your hat and hold it against the tree with the back of your left hand. Now grasp your gun and aim. You'll find that you have a nearly dead-solid hold and that you can get the shot off almost instantly. (Why the hat? Because you can take the skin off the back of your hand if you don't have something to cushion it.)

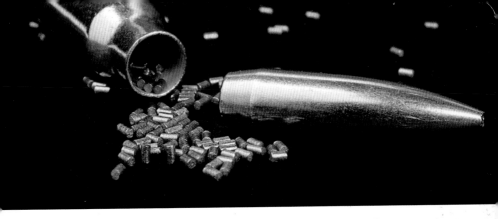

79 KNOW YOUR AMMO

The first thing you need to do is choose the right kind of ammo for your gun, but that won't be enough on its own. You also need to test out your top pick.

COMPARE BULLETS Never assume that one brand of ammo will shoot the same as another or that two different bullets of the same weight will shoot the same. I once gathered many different brands and bullet weights of .30/06 ammo and fired them in a very accurate rifle without changing the rifle's zero. When I was done, the target looked as if I had hosed it down with a machine gun. Bullets went everywhere. The fact is, some rifles are wildly inaccurate with certain loads and Tack Drivers with others. Some will shoot only one load, period. I have a .270 that will shoot only the old Trophy Bonded bullets that were made in Houston back in the 1980s. I would never sell that rifle because it is Death Its Own Self, but I'd never trust it with any other kind of bullets, either.

SHOOT GROUPS I recently watched a fellow sight in his rifle for a competition shoot. He fired a shot. Then he cranked the dials. He did this 10 times in a row: blam, crank, ka-pow, twirl, bang, twist. Later, I got to score his target, and he was all over the place because he broke a cardinal rule of sighting in: One shot tells you nothing. You need at least a three-shot group. Only after determining where the center of that group is should you make compensating windage and elevation adjustments. Then repeat until you're dead on.

80 REST EASY (BUT NOT TOO EASY)

When you sight in, you have to do it on a rest that is firm but not hard. If the fore-end is sitting on a hard surface, it will bounce at the shot, sending your bullet high. If you'd really like to get a false zero, you can rest the barrel on something—it doesn't matter whether it's hard, soft, or pleasingly firm—your bullets are going for a ride upward. It also pays to rest the fore-end at exactly the same place for each shot. In other words, don't have it resting nearly at the sling swivel for one round and near the floorplate for the next. That breeds inconsistency. And some rifles are very fussy about their preferred degree of firmness. I've owned numerous guns that I could not shoot accurately over a hard sandbag because they'd bounce. Only a softer sandbag would make them happy.

81 SHOOT GROUPS RIGHT

Nowadays, just about everyone uses three-shot groups as their standard of performance, the theory being that three is the minimum number of rounds required to see what is what, and that few big-game animals are going to stand around for more than three rounds anyway.

If you really want to see how your rifle will shoot, however, try five-shot groups. This was the standard number a couple of generations ago and is still used by target and varmint shooters whose need for consistent accuracy is more pressing. A five-shot minute-of-angle group is much more difficult to shoot than a minute-of-angle three-shotter.

And if you go back before World War II, people used 10-shot groups to measure rifle accuracy. They was men back then.

Want to measure your groups accurately? You'll need a caliper (digital-readout calipers are much easier to use than dial-readout models) and the ability to subtract. First, measure the outside spread of the two widest shots in the group. Then, subtract from that figure the diameter of the bullet you're shooting. Let's say you take your .270 and shoot a group that measures 1.313 inches. Subtract from it .277, which is the actual diameter of the bullet, and you get 1.036 inches, which is your group size.

82 KEEP COOL

As rifle barrels heat up, two things will happen to them—both bad. First, any stresses that are present in the steel will cause the tubes to warp. And second, you will create a mirage from the heat that rises off the barrel, causing you to see your groups as being higher than they are. If you shoot a Magnum rifle, or a rifle of any caliber with a lightweight barrel, you are going to have problems with overheating. Fire no more than three shots at a time and let the barrel cool to where it is no hotter than tepid (it's way too hot if you can't hold on to it and count to 10) before you continue. I've found it useful to bring two or three guns to the range. This lets me shoot one while the others are cooling. (You don't have three rifles, you say? Buy until you do.) If there's an electric outlet near the firing line, plug in a fan and let its breezes cool your barrel's fevered brow. To really make certain of where your rifle is shooting, try this as a final step: After you've sighted it in over a rest, shoot from the prone or any other position whereby you get your hand on the fore-end as you will in the field. If you use a sling to shoot when you hunt, use it now. The same applies to bipods or any other kind of support that you might rely on. Now shoot a group and see where it hits. You may need to make a few changes. Picky? You bet. But picky people make the best rifle shots.

PETZAL ON: GETTING ANTSY

"I witnessed my all-time favorite sighting screw-up on safari in Africa in 1978. A group member whined perpetually about the trackers, the game, and his rifle's alleged inability to hold its zero. The professional hunter did not appreciate the nonstop bitching at all, and finally he had had enough. 'Tom,' he said sweetly, 'I think you should resight your rifle again. Why don't you rest it on that little hill there and shoot at that mopane-tree knot?' The hill he pointed to was a safari-ant apartment complex, and when its residents were serenaded by the bellowing crack of a .375 H&H, they decided on payback. In the best safari-ant tradition, they swarmed into Tom's clothing and, at the same precise instant, started biting."

83 DRY FIRE YOUR WAY TO SUCCESS

One of the most useful tools in the ongoing struggle to shoot well is dry firing—aiming and snapping the trigger with no ammo in the chamber. Dry firing had no greater champion than the late Creighton Audette, a gunsmith, a friend of mine, and a high-power competitor who was good enough to shoot on the Palma Team and coach it. "Recoil," he said, "is a form of distraction."

He believed that any serious shooter should do far more dry firing than practicing with live ammo. (Creighton also told me once, "Everyone should have at least one gun the government doesn't know about," if you need any further proof of his wisdom.)

The Marine Corps used to start its marksmanship training with a solid week of nothing but "snapping in"—dry fire

from the basic shooting positions—to show the maggots how to do things correctly before they got live ammo. Dry fire allows you to concentrate, without distraction, on that moment when the trigger lets go and the instant immediately afterward, when so many other things can end up going wrong.

Dry fire, however, is not for every firearm. It's okay to dry fire most bolt-action rifles, but the practice can damage most .22s, just about all shotguns, and some handguns. If you are in doubt about its effect on your firearms, you should consult your gunsmith.

It costs nothing, won't give you a flinch, and makes no noise. Dry fire a lot and you will shoot better. As Ed Zern said, "Keep your powder, your martinis, your trout flies, and your fire dry."

QUICK SHOT

84 DRESS TO KILL

To ensure a rifle's scope is correctly mounted, put on the clothes you'll wear while hunting (including a heavy coat if needed). With the scope loose in the rings, set it on a low power. Close your eyes and throw the gun to your shoulder. Now open your eyes. You should see the full field of view, and the scope's ocular lens should be 4 inches from your eyebrow. If not, adjust it until you get the right distance, and then tighten the rings.

85 LEARN TRIGGER CONTROL

Your trigger should break at no less than 3 pounds, no more than 4, and at the same weight every time. It should not creep at all, and should have an absolute minimum of overtravel as well.

That said, when you acquire your sight picture, take a deep breath and let most of it out. You now have 7 seconds in which to shoot. If you don't, your vision begins to deteriorate, and you have to start all over again, which can cost you a shot. So, you should discipline yourself to aim and get the round off forthwith. Screw around, and you'll miss.

It's common advice that you should squeeze the trigger so that you're surprised when the rifle goes off. This assumes you can hold the rifle perfectly still. I can't do

that in the field. I wobble and weave—not much, but enough. Instead, I pick the precise instant when the crosshairs are where they should be and then pull that trigger smartly.

If you have a bolt-action centerfire, you can work on your trigger pull by dry firing. After making sure your rifle is unloaded, pick out a target 50 yards or so away and practice getting the rifle to your shoulder, acquiring the perfect sight picture, and pulling that trigger, over and over. But be discreet about this. If your neighbors see you aiming a rifle out your window, you will shortly get a visit from the local SWAT team, who will inquire, politely but firmly, what you're up to. After they fire a warning shot through your heart.

86
HEAR WHAT YOUR RIFLE IS TELLING YOU

Were this the best of all possible worlds, we would fire three rifle shots at a target, peer downrange, and see three holes clustered within the area of a dime at precisely the right place. But this is not the best of all possible worlds, in that it has a place for chiggers, bad cholesterol, rabies, and abdominal fat. And in this vale of sorrow, we often look at our targets and see nothing but horror, chaos, and disorder.

In any event, we know that something is wrong, but what? Rather than bursting into tears, you should regard this as a heart-to-heart talk with your rifle, which, if you can speak its language, will tell you what ails it.

DIAGNOSTIC TOOL
Shooting from the benchrest will tell you just what your gun is thinking.

COMPLETE BREAKDOWN
Problem Your shots are all over the place, and you can't get a group to save your life. There could be several causes. First is a ruptured scope. The way to test this is to put a different scope on your gun and see if it groups better. Second is loose bedding screws on the rifle. Check to see if they're tight. Third is loose ring or base screws. Sometimes, one particular bullet weight will give results this bad. If this is the case, it's usually because the barrel's rifling twist is wrong for that bullet weight.

CONSISTENT FLIER
Problem Your ammo is almost, but not quite, right for your gun. Usually this shows up as two holes close together and the third one off to the side by an inch or two. At 100 yards, this is not a problem, but at farther distances, it will begin to cause some trouble. It's caused by bullets traveling just above or below the optimum speed for that barrel, causing it to vibrate inconsistently. Handloaders can cure it by raising or lowering the powder charge. Non-handloaders will have to try different ammunition.

INCONSISTENT FLIER
Problem Most of the time you get good groups, but sometimes you have one shot go astray, and then sometimes all three go where they're not supposed to. Most likely you're flinching, and if you don't think that it's possible to flinch from a benchrest, think again. You can buy or experiment with a sled-type shooting rest, which can virtually eliminate felt recoil, or try putting a soft gun case or sandbag between your shoulder and the butt. Or, if all else fails, get a less punishing rifle.

RISING GROUP
Problem Your groups are usually okay, but they seem to keep moving up on the target, sometimes up and to the left or right, sometimes straight up. This is caused by an overheated barrel. When a tube gets too hot, it warps slightly, sending bullets errantly, and, in addition, the heat waves rising from it give you a distorted view of the target, sort of like shooting through a swimming pool. The cure is easy: Let your barrel cool down. Start each group with a cold barrel and never let it get beyond lukewarm.

STRINGING
Problem In this situation, your groups string vertically or horizontally. First check the barrel bedding. Most barrels today are free-floating; there should be no contact from $1\frac{1}{2}$ inches forward of the receiver right out to the end. If there is, take the gun in for a rebedding job. The horizontal grouping can be caused by wind at the target that you don't feel at the bench. The vertical groups can be caused by the fore-end jumping on too hard a surface.

87 WATCH YOUR FORM

Much of proper rifle-shooting technique is designed to spare you pain, and if you simply pick up a gun and start blazing away, you are going to take some needless punishment. For example, if you don't get the butt into the "pocket" that forms when you raise your right arm to shoulder the rifle, it is going to ride out on your bicep and pound you. If you lean back from the waist to support the gun's weight (women are especially guilty of this), you will be rocked back on your heels. If you crawl the stock, the scope will sooner or later say hello to your forehead. Get competent help. A range officer or an NRA instructor can assist you. A shooting class will also work wonders.

88 LEARN TO TAKE A PUNCH

When the great welterweight boxer Tommy Hearns was just starting to learn the manly art, he was sparring with a much better fighter who promptly broke his nose. Hearns grabbed his nose with his glove, wrenched it back in place, and kept right on fighting. Some people are much tougher than others, and just as the Motor City Cobra could ignore a busted beak, some of us can take a lot more recoil than others. There are two types: real recoil, measured in foot-pounds; and perceived recoil, what you feel. There is a formula for calculating real recoil, but it's easier to go online and find any of the several sites that can do it with the click of a mouse. Perceived recoil is affected by the makeup and design of the rifle, and it can't really be calculated.

One of the most sadistic rifles ever built was the Winchester Model 95 lever action. The majority were made in .30/06 and .30/40 Krag, and a fair number used the .405 Winchester. The 95 had all the requirements for a truly painful rifle. Its stock had loads of drop, so that when it recoiled, the barrel whipped up and back, directing much of the recoil into the shooter's head. The stock's comb was sharp, guaranteeing a bruised cheekbone, and the butt was small, curved, and capped by a steel plate, ensuring the maximum amount of hurt in your shoulder. In .30/40, which is a mild-kicking cartridge, and in .30/06, which is moderate, the Model 95 was brutal. In .405 it must have been unthinkable. Muzzle blast is not physically connected to recoil but can also seem to make a rifle kick harder. You can develop a raging flinch from shooting a muzzle-braked rifle or a short-barreled rifle without hearing protection. You'll swear it kicks like a mule even though it doesn't. Your build is also a factor: Recoil flings around small, slender people in a spine-chilling manner. But they are actually suffering less than heavyset people because they give with the shove, whereas the fire-hydrant types soak up every bit of it. Of the people I know who have been permanently screwed up by kick, all of them are close to 6 feet in height and weigh more than 180 pounds—not a lightweight in the lot.

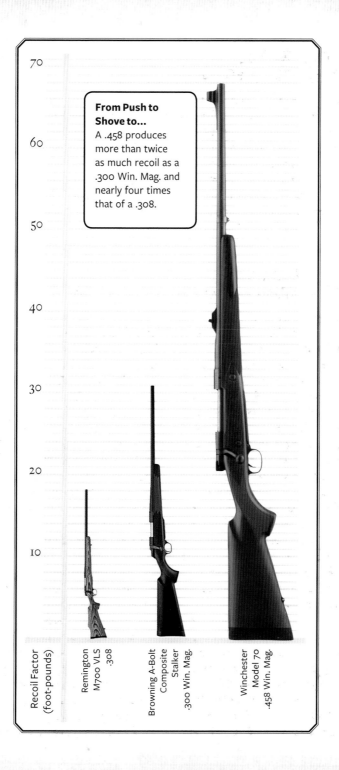

From Push to Shove to...
A .458 produces more than twice as much recoil as a .300 Win. Mag. and nearly four times that of a .308.

70

60

50

40

30

20

10

Recoil Factor
(foot-pounds)

Remington
M700 VLS
.308

Browning A-Bolt
Composite
Stalker
.300 Win. Mag.

Winchester
Model 70
.458 Win. Mag.

89 LOWER THE KICK

In case you're really suffering the pain of recoil, here are some things that will bring you instant relief.

RECOIL PAD Get rid of your aluminum or hard-plastic buttplate or your cheap, unyielding-as-granite factory recoil pad and replace it with a soft, squishy, premium recoil pad.

MUZZLE BRAKE They're not cheap, they'll rip your ears to shreds if you're not plugged and muffed, and you'll need to have a gunsmith do the work, but they really do save you a lot of foot-pounds. Some shooters opt to have Mag-na-ports cut in their barrel. This will reduce muzzle jump but not recoil, and bullet jacket fouling tends to collect at the rear corners of the ports, eventually cutting down on accuracy.

STOCK If you have an older rifle with loads of drop at the comb, get a more modern stock with a lot less drop. Unless your rifle is extremely rare or odd, you can choose among wood, laminated wood, and synthetic stocks. See your gunsmith.

INERTIA RECOIL REDUCER Have a gunsmith install one (or better yet, a pair of them) in your stock. They will change the balance of your rifle and increase its weight by about a pound, but they work.

TRIGGER A heavy trigger pull will add greatly to the unpleasantness of a hard-kicking rifle. A light, crisp trigger will make it easier to set the thing off, thus rendering the whole experience more tolerable. Don't even think about diddling with a trigger. Take it to a gunsmith who can alter or, if necessary, replace it.

90 KNOW YOUR LIMITS

For most shooters, the cutoff for real recoil is around the .30/06 or 7mm Remington Magnum level, which is about 25 foot-pounds. When you add 10 foot-pounds, the average shooter really feels it—and as a result, he will not shoot the rifle very well.

There is a huge divide between the .375 H&H and the .40-caliber and larger rounds. I believe a considerable number of shooters can't or shouldn't shoot anything bigger than a .375. My own personal limit is the .458 Lott. Bigger rifles exist: The .460 Weatherby, for example, develops just over 100 foot-pounds. I have shot one on several occasions, but I'm not about to do so anymore.

Here are some approximate figures for nine popular cartridges. All weights are for the rifle alone; a scope and mounts will add about a pound, and the recoil will decrease proportionately.

Cartridge	Rifle Weight (lb.)	Recoil (ft.-lb.)
.243	7	12
.270	7.5	21
.30/30	7.5	10.5
.308	7.5	18
.30/06	8	24
7mm Rem. Mag.	8	27
.300 Win. Mag.	8.5	31
.338	9	35
.375 H&H	9.5	39

PETZAL ON: FEAR

❝ Don't ever fall for one of the more pervasive myths in riflery, which goes: 'Even if you flinch when you're shooting at targets, you won't flinch when you're shooting at game because you won't feel the recoil.' If you are afraid of a particular gun, you are going to stay afraid of it, and you'll miss. Period.❞

91 SHOOT LIKE A MARKSMAN

Once upon a time, someone asked Willie Mays how he hit so well, and the Say Hey Kid said that you watched the ball come to you, as big as a pumpkin, and you just put the bat in the middle of it. Now if you've ever seen a fastball come at you at 90 mph plus, you know that it looks like a kid's aspirin tablet—if you can see the thing at all. But Mays was gifted. He did with amazing ease what most normal people can't do at all.

Depressingly, in the world of rifle shooting, there are people just like him. A friend of mine, a marksman of the first order, once competed against Gary Anderson, who was one of the great American rifle shots of the 20th century. My friend summed up the experience thus: "I didn't think it was possible to be beaten that badly." Anderson, of course, was supremely gifted. But what if Nature has not lavished her gifts on you? No sense in worrying about it; there's no use worrying about it. But you can get a lot more improvement by applying some basic fundamentals of marksmanship, which far too many hunters don't bother with.

Though some shooters tout the need for upper-body strength in order to shoot well, the ability to bench-press 300 pounds won't make you a better shot. Far better is the ability to make your hands do what the eyes and brain tell them to. This hand-eye coordination is the same quality that makes for good Ping-Pong players and skilled golfers.

It's pretty simple: First, learn to shoot correctly. Then, practice. A lot.

92 DOPE THE WIND

There are all sorts of devices that will tell you how far away something is or what your holdover should be, but nothing that scopes out the breezes that make your life a waking hell. So, filled with despair, I offer these rules.

LOOK AHEAD Don't worry about what the wind is doing where you are; watch it midway to the target.

FLY RIGHT The faster a bullet is moving, the less the wind pushes it. The heavier and more streamlined it is, the less the wind pushes it. This doesn't apply to short, fat bullets—despite their weight, they don't slip easily through the air.

INCH CLOSER It's easy to outsmart yourself by holding off too much. If you have wind-resistant bullets and lots of velocity and are not shooting from terribly far away (say, 250 yards or less), then a moderate wind is going to push your slug a couple of inches one way or another, but no more than that.

93 SHOOT FASTER

In Montana in the early '80s, I was hunting a ridgeline in deep, soft snow and jumped a nice whitetail buck out of his bed. He whirled and started to accelerate, and I had perhaps two seconds to get my rifle up, find him in the scope, figure out the lead, and pull the trigger. As it was, two seconds was enough, and he was the only deer I saw that whole trip.

In the best of all possible worlds, we would be able to watch a critter stroll into view, raise our rifles in a leisurely manner, and shoot with all the time we need. In this world, we are sometimes forced to shoot at an animal that is about to get, or is getting, the hell out of there—or we end up going home empty-handed.

(And before we go any further, you should understand that I'm not presenting you with a rationale to blaze away at anything you please. Speed becomes a factor only after you've identified your target beyond the shadow of a doubt. If you're not sure of it, keep your rifle down and watch through your binoculars until you are.) Here are the basics.

DEFEAT DITHER Speed is achieved by the absence of dither—a brew concocted from indecision and clumsiness that saves thousands of animals' lives every year. Much indecision comes from not knowing clearly what you want to shoot. "Should I settle for a forkhorn? What if a better deer comes along after I shoot this one?" While you are debating, the deer becomes aware of you and leaves. Decide what you want beforehand, and stick to your decision.

TAKE THE SHOTS YOU CAN MAKE If you think you can't make a shot, you are probably right. As you become experienced, you will develop a very good sense of which shots you can take and which you can't. Until you reach that point, play it cautious.

KNOW YOUR RIFLE Much hesitation is caused by unfamiliarity with your firearm. "Omigod, where's the safety on this thing?" If you have a new rifle, or a different action from what you're used to, or you only pick up your rifle once a year, you will dither—unless you practice.

94 DEVELOP A SENSE OF TIMING

It's important to learn to distinguish between those times when you have to shoot fast and those when you can take your time. Many shots are missed because hunters are slow or because they panic. What to do? Use your common sense. If an animal is right under your tree stand, it can get your scent at any instant, and you are going to have to shoot right now. If it's 300 yards away, you're not likely to have your cover blown unless you stand up and cheer. Also, look at the critter. Animals have body language that reveals whether they're spooked or placid.

If a deer stamps with a front hoof, he has you spotted and is trying to get you to do something stupid.

If the tail comes up, that tells you that he is leaving right now.

A deer puts his head down and pretends to feed, then yanks it up to see if anything is going on. Let him do this a few times, and he'll settle down.

95 LEARN TO SWITCH HIT

On more than one occasion, I've had to endure the shame of shooting right-handed when I was up in a tree stand and a deer came from my left-hand side. Since I shoot southpaw, I couldn't turn enough to aim at him without getting busted, so I moved the butt of the rifle into my right shoulder and shot that way. If you have a strong dominant eye on your shooting side, you are going to have to close it to shoot from the weak side. As shown for a right-hander, switching sides lets you cover everything in front of you. Plenty of practice helps.

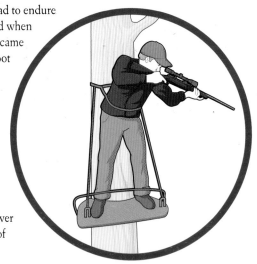

96 DRILL FOR SPEED

I'm sluggish and torpid by nature, so by rights I should never get fast-breaking game. However, for 25 years, I've practiced shooting quickly every chance I get. This drill will help you do the same.

The drill consists of two parts. At home, I practice shouldering a rifle that I've checked very carefully to make sure is unloaded, aiming at a lichen patch on an oak tree 50 yards away and snapping the trigger, all in as close to one motion as I can make it. Do this regularly, and you'll get pretty fast and pretty smooth. Don't do this if you live where the neighbors can see you. You'll be visited by a SWAT team, and you'll get to see just how fast they can shoot instead.

Then, at a 100-yard range, I put up a target with an 8-inch bull and load five rounds. I shoulder the rifle, aim, and allow myself 3 seconds to get off the shot. If I can't get the crosshairs where I want them in that time, I lower the rifle and count it as a miss. (If you shoot at a public range, check first to make sure this kind of practice is permitted.)

Hits that go anywhere inside the black count; anything outside the black is a miss. I go through 20 rounds, and if I can put at least 18 bullets through the black, I'm doing okay, provided that the other two are no farther out of the bull than the nine-ring. Speed kills—and it also puts venison on your table.

97 PERFECT THE UPSIDE-DOWN CARRY

There is a way to sling a rifle that allows you to bring it into action quickly and use the sling as a shooting support at the same time. In the past, when I've recommended this technique, I've set all the Safety Nazis in a frenzy. To them I say: "One hand is always on the rifle and has it under constant control." It's not as though the gun is swinging freely, doing whatever it pleases. I learned how to do this in 1958 from a gun writer named Francis E. Sell, who had probably used it for 50 years at that point. I have been using it for 46 years. Sell did not shoot himself in all that time, and neither have I, so spare me.

It works like this: Assuming you have a smooth rifle sling and not one of the grabby kind that won't slip off your shoulder, and assuming you're left-handed, you sling the rifle over your right shoulder, muzzle down, trigger guard forward. Your right hand should be on the fore-end to control the movement of the gun.

When it comes time to shoot, you simply haul the rifle up and put the butt in your left shoulder. The sling remains looped around the upper part of your left arm as a brace. This can be done in one motion with a minimum of movement and is very fast. And as the signs correctly say, speed kills.

98 UNSLING IT

Rifle slings have saved the lives of more critters than PETA. Used incorrectly, a sling (or more properly, a carrying strap) can place your rifle out of reach for more than enough time for an animal to bolt and die of old age.

Sling misuse can have even more serious consequences. Many years ago, I was on the trail of a highly irritated lion in the Kalahari Desert of Botswana, .375 slung over my shoulder. Ian Manning, the professional hunter whose job it was to keep me from becoming lion poop, said, "David, do you really think the bloody lion is going to wait for you to unsling your bloody rifle before he

bites you in your bloody arse?" I had offered to fight Manning the day before when he said my rifle looked like it belonged to a French nobleman, but there was no doubt he was making sense about the sling.

The only situations in which your rifle should be slung is when you have no intention of shooting anything or when you have to use both hands for something. (You should not sling a rifle while getting into a tree stand; instead, get in the stand first, then pull the unloaded gun up with a rope.) The rest of the time, put the sling in your pocket and be ready to shoot.

99 PROTECT YOUR RIFLE FROM THE ELEMENTS

The worst-case scenario for rifles is if you get snow or ice in the bore. This will put your gun out of action. Firing a rifle or shotgun with a plugged bore will get you a new nickname—Stumpy, for example. The way to prevent this is to cover the muzzle with just a small piece of plastic electricians' tape or bowhunters' camo tape. I've had people assure me that this will blow up the rifle, but it's perfectly safe as long as you observe two precautions:

One, don't use heavy tape. Two, don't let condensation form in the barrel. If the condensation freezes, you have trouble. If you're going to expose the rifle to drastic temperature changes, take off the tape and air out the barrel.

Rifles rust, including stainless-steel rifles; they just rust slower than blued steel. The solution: Wipe the metal down with an oily rag at the end of the day. Pay particular attention to the bolt, which is bright metal and prone to rust. If you're hunting in a dry climate, such as in the Rockies, rust doesn't seem to occur, no matter what the weather is. But elsewhere, beware.

The trigger can be an especially vulnerable part of your rifle. I've seen at least a couple of triggers that were ruined by rust from being wet day after day. The temptation is to put oil on the trigger, but you will regret doing this, as the oil will eventually congeal, and your trigger will cease to move.

The proper course is to remove the bolt and squirt the trigger from above with lighter fluid, being sure to hit the sear. Do this every time the rifle gets soaked. This appears to flush out whatever water lies lurking. Also, while the bolt is out of the rifle, wipe it down with a lightly oiled rag and do the same with the bolt raceway.

As for the rest of the metal, don't worry about it. Getting at it requires that you remove the barreled action from the stock, and unless you know for a fact that the gun will shoot to the same point of impact when screwed together, let it be.

Another thing you must not do is put your wet rifle in a case. This practically guarantees rust. Dry it off completely and then put it in a case.

100 COPE WITH BAD WEATHER

One of my more vivid memories of the army is standing in a driving sleet storm watching the warm ugh in my mess tray turning rapidly to cold, congealed ugh and thinking that when I left the Green Machine I was never going to stand around in the sleet again. And so I left the service, took up big-game hunting, and have stood around in sleet—and much worse—forever after.

Cold, wet weather can not only affect the stuff on your mess tray; it can affect you, your gear, your scope, and your rifle. Let's start with you. That's easy. If you dress wrong in inclement weather, you will become hypothermic and die. Your rifle—that's a bit more complicated. The army looked very unkindly on a rusted rifle, and we learned that, above all, you took care of your weapon (not your gun, thank you very much) first, no matter what kind of shape you yourself were in. Finding rust on a rifle was enough to get you a long night on duty in the mess hall, scrubbing out pots and pans, which, for sheer loathsomeness, could only compare to a contemporary political campaign. Much better to take proper care of your rifle, we were told, because only then would it take care of you.

101 KEEP YOUR POWDER DRY (OR NOT)

Ammo, unlike you, is almost impervious to water. On many occasions I have had the same three cartridges in my magazine through a week of torrential rain and have never had a round fail to fire. Modern smokeless powder is nonhygroscopic, meaning it won't absorb water.

About 15 years ago, a friend of mine who was a shipwreck nut brought me a couple of rounds of .30/06 military ammo that had been aboard the *USS San Diego* when that ship was torpedoed off the New Jersey coast in the early days of World War II. These cartridges had lain beneath the Atlantic Ocean for 40-plus years, and their cases were so badly corroded that I could punch a hole in one with my fingernail and pour out the powder. Which I did. I then put some in an ashtray, touched a match to it, and it flared right up.

If you handload, and you're worried about water, you can buy a cartridge-sealing adhesive from Loc-Tite. But, really, it isn't necessary. Mike Jordan of Winchester says that his company seals military ammunition (which has to pass an immersion test) and the primers of handgun ammo (which is used by cops and other people who shoot people) but that their hunting-rifle ammo is unsealed, and it doesn't leak either.

INDEX

ABOUT THE AUTHOR

DAVID E. PETZAL is the Rifles Field Editor of *Field & Stream*. He has been with the publication since 1972. A graduate of Colgate University, he served in the US Army from 1963 to 1969, and he began writing about rifles and rifle shooting in 1964, during his service. He is a Benefactor Member of the National Rifle Association and a Life Member of the Amateur Trapshooting Association. He has hunted all over the United States and Canada, as well as in Europe, Africa, and New Zealand.

Petzal wrote *The .22 Rifle* and edited *The Encyclopedia of Sporting Firearms*. In 2002, he was awarded the Leupold Jack Slack Writer of the Year Award, and in 2005 he received the Zeiss Outdoor Writer of the Year Award, making him the first person to win both. His writing ability and knowledge of firearms are often referred to as "godlike."

FROM THE AUTHOR

I would like to thank everyone with whom I have ever hunted or shot, because I've learned from all of you.

IMAGE CREDITS

FIELD & STREAM

Editor Anthony Licata
VP, Group Publisher Eric Zinczenko

2 Park Avenue
New York, NY 10016
www.fieldandstream.com

weldonowen

President, CEO Terry Newell
VP, Publisher Roger Shaw
Executive Editor Mariah Bear
Editorial Assistant Ian Cannon
Creative Director Kelly Booth
Art Director Barbara Genetin
Designer Michel Gadwa
Cover Design William Mack
Illustration Coordinator Conor Buckley
Production Director Chris Hemesath
Production Manager Michelle Duggan

All of the material in this book was originally
published in *The Total Gun Manual*, by David E.
Petzal and Phil Bourjaily.

Weldon Owen would like to thank William Mack for
the original design concept, which was adapted from
The Total Gun Manual. Marisa Solís and Bridget
Fitzgerald provided editorial assistance.

© 2013 Weldon Owen Inc.

415 Jackson Street
San Francisco, CA 94111
www.weldonowen.com

Field & Stream and Weldon Owen are divisions of
BONNIER

Library of Congress Control Number on file with the
publisher.

ISBN 13: 978-1-61628-486-2
ISBN 10: 1-61628-486-2

10 9 8 7 6 5 4 3 2 1

2012 2013 2014 2015

Printed in China by 1010